Sweet Relief

The Marla Ruzicka Story

By Jennifer Abrahamson

SIMON SPOTLIGHT ENTERTAINMENT
NEW YORK • LONDON • TORONTO • SYDNEY

SSE

SIMON SPOTLIGHT ENTERTAINMENT
An imprint of Simon & Schuster
1230 Avenue of the Americas, New York, New York 10020
Text copyright © 2006 by Jennifer Abrahamson
Designed by Steve Kennedy
Manufactured in the U.S.A.
First Edition
2 4 6 8 10 9 7 5 3 1
Library of Congress Cataloging-in-Publication Data
Abrahamson, Jennifer.
Sweet relief: the Marla Ruzicka story / by Jennifer Abrahamson. —1st ed.
p. cm.
ISBN-13: 978-1-4169-1778-6   ISBN-10: 1-4169-1778-0
1. Ruzicka, Marla, 1976–2005. 2. Social reformers—Unites States—Biography.
3. Political activists—United States—Biography. 4. Iraq War, 2003—Biography. I. Title.
HN57.A547 2006   956.7044'31092—dc22   [B]
2006021269

For Marla

Contents

Prologue

April 16, 2005, Marla Ruzicka and Faiz Ali Salim were traveling along the most lethal seven miles of concrete on Earth, Baghdad's Airport Road. Marla wore a full-body *abaya* veil, despite the shimmering heat. Faiz's hands gripped the steering wheel as his eyes scanned the other cars.

Marla had called her journalist friend Colin McMahon on the phone earlier. She told him about a successful meeting she had had in the Green Zone, the fortified home to the new Iraqi government and the U.S. Embassy, and she promised to return quickly to the safety of the Al-Hamra Hotel. She was organizing one of her famous parties that evening at the journalist hub. Before heading back, she wanted to squeeze in one more important stop. Marla didn't tell Colin where.

Did she visit an Iraqi family who had suffered casualties during the war? Some of the residents living in the communities accessible only by Airport Road had lost children, wives, limbs, and homes during the U.S. advance on Baghdad and subsequent warfare. The mission of Campaign for Innocent

Victims in Conflict (CIVIC), the organization Marla had founded, was to help such casualties of war. Her work required frequent trips to their villages and neighborhoods. However, it is possible that she wasn't visiting with families at all that day. Her earlier triumph in the Green Zone suggests that she might have gone to one of the U.S. military facilities near the airport. There, she would talk to an army contact about people killed or injured by U.S. firepower.

Friends and family implored her to be careful in Baghdad. Two days before, Marla wrote an e-mail to her loved ones.

Hello,

Just a quick note to say that Faiz (who runs CIVIC in Iraq) and I are safe. Today, there were some car bombs that exploded close to where I stay, but we are very much protected in the compound where I live. At the time, I was in the Green Zone meeting with a senior official from the Ministry of Human Rights.

I will leave early next week. It will be hard because we are doing tremendous work and solving many problems. I am very safe. However, I know when you hear news of kidnappings and bombs, it does not put your mind at ease, so I wanted to assure you that I am fine and exercising good judgment—to borrow a quote from my dad.

Lots of love, Marla

Between 2:45 and 3:00 in the afternoon, Faiz navigated their unarmored sedan down the highway toward Baghdad. Most likely, Marla's head was darting back and forth, her platinum blond hair swishing against the *abaya*'s black cloth. She was undoubtedly brainstorming new ideas on how to win aid for war victims. In an effort to calm Faiz, she would have offered a compliment about his infant daughter, followed by her gravelly giggle.

Marla was undoubtedly yammering away in the passenger seat, maybe while fishing for a brush in her big black bag, when they were forced to slow down behind a large military patrol rumbling down the road. For security reasons, the military prohibited most civilian traffic from passing, but a convoy of American government contractors were waved through by the patrol, and they began passing Faiz and Marla. Perhaps Marla was then thinking about the beaches of Thailand, where she would get some much needed R & R in a few days' time. A car drove up beside them in the next lane. Intending to strike the convoy, the man driving next to the pair detonated his bomb, and Marla and Faiz's car burst into flames. Bearing the brunt of the hit, Faiz burned to death. A U.S. Army medic rushed to the scene and hovered over Marla, who was lying on the road near the smoldering wreckage. When she regained consciousness, she managed just two words: "I'm alive."

I was late meeting a friend for Sunday brunch in Brooklyn. As I waited for the F train on the open-air platform, my cell phone rang. It was my mother calling from California. She was watching CNN.

"Marla's been killed," she said.

In the days that followed, hundreds of messages from names both familiar and foreign clogged my inbox. There was a flurry of phone calls and visits from journalists seeking quotes for stories about Marla's life and death. I vaguely remember interviewing with a radio network on my cell phone in the bathroom of a Brooklyn bar, where I'd met up with a few of Marla's other friends after hearing the horrifying news. Not knowing what else to do, we sat together, dazed, making phone calls.

A few days later I started on a familiar journey along the bends and curves of the road that led me from the San Francisco Bay Area, where I had grown up, to my family's lakeside cabin.

My mind turned to Marla. How many times had she driven on this same road, returning from another adventure in a far-off land? Had she welcomed the familiar scenery with the same hunger?

Now I was driving alone in a rented car to Clear Lake, a journey that normally ended in joy and excitement, but today would deliver me to a place of pain and sorrow—Marla's funeral.

Gravel crunched under tires as I turned into our driveway and came to a stop. Marla's parents were holding a pre-funeral gathering for close friends and family at their home across the lake. Before heading over, I poured myself a glass of wine and walked outside.

A blue heron spread its wings and lumbered off the dock and into the sky. Storm clouds began to gather over the lake, turning it gray, and the wind kicked up fresh whitecaps. As the rain began to fall, I remembered the first time I met Marla, so far away from our lake's cool waters.

I was about to become a media spokesperson for the United Nations World Food Program's Afghanistan operation, which was attempting to feed half of the country's civilian population in the months after the United States drove the Taliban government from power in late 2001. I knew not a soul in the country and not nearly enough about the crisis. Shortly before leaving for Kabul in February 2002, my colleagues in Islamabad, Pakistan, told me to keep an eye out for a Californian woman called Marla with "wild blond hair." In Afghanistan, Marla was ubiquitous. She was at every party and every news conference. She was the most recognizable member of a community of foreign correspondents and aid workers who popped up at the most unpredictable times. I pressed further. Did she have a last name? Smiling secretively, they simply assured me that she was a good person to talk to.

A few days after my arrival, I was lunching at the United Nations guest house in Kabul when a journalist entered looking for Marla. I hadn't met her yet, but offered to pass on a message if she materialized.

The second Marla stumbled into the room I knew it was her. She twisted and turned her mussed blond head as if she were looking for somebody. A collection of tattered folders jutted out from her arms at different angles. She was wearing something heavy—either a suede Pakistani coat or an Afghan vest—with a ragged fur collar. There were thick half moons of dirt beneath her fingernails. She was an almost waiflike Dickensian street urchin.

"You must be Marla," I said.

She spun around and her dark eyes fixed on me impatiently. I passed on the journalist's message and her expression warmed. Thanking me, she disappeared through the door.

Two weeks later, a handful of spokespeople from various UN agencies gathered at a shabby conference hall in Kabul to update the foreign press corps on the country's humanitarian situation. I arrived at the UN compound early on that cold March day, nervous about my presentation. Loitering outside the building, I saw Marla standing close by.

"Hi, sweetie, how are *you*?" she greeted the mostly male journalists as they filed into the conference room.

I wasn't quite sure why she was there. She appeared to be crashing the press briefing to do some networking. I should have been the one welcoming the reporters, but Marla took center stage. Despite her self-assuredness, the bubbly girl seemed completely out of place in a sea of cynical, war-seasoned journalists. She reminded me of a college sophomore about to lead a pep rally more than a human rights worker. Seemingly naive, Marla readily offered smiles and giggles to anyone who listened. As a perky blonde in Afghanistan, it wasn't hard to find an audience.

We struck up a conversation. She spoke in loud California tones, and her speech was interspersed with "dude," "cool," and "you totally rock!" A bandanna reined in her wild hair. She told me she was the sole Afghanistan representative for Global Exchange, an activist group based in San Francisco. Excited to meet someone from home, I told her I was also from northern California. She immediately warmed to me, as if we were long-lost friends. We kept talking, and she revealed that she was from Lakeport, a straight shot across Clear Lake from my family's summer cabin. Lakeport is a place where doors are left unlocked at night and last names are an afterthought. The town is three hours northeast of San Francisco, tucked between the vineyards of Napa Valley to the south and thickly forested hills stretching west to the Pacific Ocean. A mile-long stretch of Main Street, lined with family-owned diners, shops, and seasonal motels, comprises the town's commercial center. Starbucks has yet to open a branch, and inquiring about an Internet café elicits only bewildered expressions from the locals.

I was floored. I'd never met anyone from conservative Lake County outside of the area, let alone halfway around the world. I wondered how she had ended up working in Afghanistan alone, with no office, no home, and little money. Over the next months and years, the pieces of the puzzle fell into place.

Chapter 1

The Wonder Years

(How to Become an Activist)

Yes the world is filled with evil and we all have hardships
but every day I love life a little more and this gives me more
faith in changing the world.
—FROM MARLA RUZICKA'S JOURNAL, UNDATED

Dozens of eighth graders streamed onto the main quad of Terrace Middle School. Their teachers looked on, speechless.

"One, two, three, four, we don't want no fucking war!" chanted the mass of teenagers. Just moments before, they had been sitting in their seats half-listening to math lessons, scribbling notes to friends, or staring out the window, daydreaming about water-skiing or a new crush.

It was January 17, 1991, the day of the first Gulf War in Iraq. Earlier that week Marla had watched the episode of *The Wonder Years* where Fred Savage's character and his friends stage a protest against the Vietnam War at their suburban school. Inspired by the television show and upset by the prospect of America's involvement in a war, Marla, who was student body president, decided to do something about it. She and her friend Hillary Golden quickly organized their fellow student body officers and classmates, recruiting them to join a school walkout in protest of Operation Desert Storm.

News of the walkout quickly spread through town. A local TV crew arrived, eager to record images of the most controversial event in memory to hit Lakeport. The cameras recorded twenty-eight seconds of footage, which showed Marla imploring her fellow students not to use the "F word."

Seventy students gathered in front of the television cameras chanting slogans and waving signs reading "Give peace a chance" and "No war." Principal Timothy Hoff threatened to remove student leaders from office if they didn't return to class. Marla walked right up to him and said she was responsible. She was taken to the principal's office as a group of her classmates pounded on the windows, demanding, "Let her go! Let her go!"

"Are you the one?" Mr. Jim Rogers asked Marla as she took her seat in the front row of his freshman English class. Wearing a sheepish grin, Marla ducked and shook her head.

"I just want to say thanks," Jim said. "It took courage to lead the walkout at Terrace."

Surprised, Marla beamed at her teacher.

Jim often encouraged thought-provoking discussions in his classroom. One day he asked his students, "Should we have dropped the atomic bomb on Japan?"

Marla whipped her hand in the air. Jim told her to go ahead.

"How many people died? Like, a hundred thousand? More? How is that right? Imagine if that was you, or all of us here in Lakeport, who were bombed. It's just wrong to kill all those innocent people. That's never okay!"

In Jim Rogers's junior year honors history and English class, Marla sometimes got so wound up with passion on a particular subject that he had to ask her to slow down. The words spilling from her lips couldn't keep pace with the speed of her mind. Marla would become so fired up that her arguments often soared over the heads of her fellow students, who didn't share her passion or ideals. Once she finished making her point, Marla slipped back into a shell of bubbly lightness.

Jim once turned a 1960s history lesson into a protest project. When it was Marla's turn, she skipped up to the front of the classroom with her group and whipped out a large, elastic bra. Laughing hysterically, she used a lighter to set it on fire.

"NO!" Jim yelled.

Ushering everyone outside, Jim then allowed it. Marla lit the bra, and the flame spewed out a toxic cloud of black smoke.

"Oh, look at Miss Environment!" her classmates joked.

"Vote for women!" she chanted, waving the singed material.

"Marla, women already had the right to vote in the sixties!" Jim said.

"No more war! No more war!" she began yelling instead, guffawing and jumping up and down.

Marla's off-the-wall personality and idealistic enthusiasm amused the town's inhabitants, who didn't take her seriously. Throughout high school, Marla challenged their conformist mindset. She started Clear Lake High's first environmental club. Appalled that there was no girls' soccer team, she canvassed the town to raise money to start one herself. When the school's student counselor was let go because of budgetary concerns, Marla proposed that she take on the role, but the school district refused. Frustrated but not discouraged, she began setting her sights beyond Lakeport to places where her ambitions would be appreciated.

Tony Newman was rushing to talk to one of his colleagues in the San Francisco–based Global Exchange offices when something strange in the reception area caught his eye. He stopped and watched a teenage girl snatching up handfuls of pamphlets.

"Can I help you with anything?" Tony asked the young blonde.

"Hi, I'm Marla!" the girl announced, flashing him a huge smile. "This is great! We don't have any of this stuff up in Lakeport. I'm going to bring it back to my school."

Tony said he'd never heard of Lakeport and asked where it was. With a wave of the hand, Marla explained that, oh, it was just outside of San Francisco. She'd read about Global Exchange and thought it sounded interesting. So she'd jumped into her iridescent blue Ford Probe—better known by Lakeport locals as the "protest-mobile," decorated with bumper stickers boasting slogans like "Mean people suck"—

and sped to San Francisco. Global Exchange, which promotes social, economic, and environmental justice around the world, was the political home Marla had dreamed of finding.

Marla asked Tony what he did for Global Exchange. He explained that he organized trips to Cuba, openly challenging the U.S. government travel ban. The group visited Cuban day-care centers, youth groups, schools, women's organizations, and hospitals as a means of forming a bond of friendship between the people of the two countries.

"That's great, that's great. Your work sounds amazing! Can you come up to Lakeport and give a talk about Cuba?" she asked.

He said he would make a presentation in Lakeport, but he thought there was maybe a twenty-five percent chance that she'd follow up on it. A couple of days later, she called and asked him if he could still come up to Lakeport.

A few days after her call, Tony and a friend started the trip. Marla had said it was just a quick drive up from San Francisco. "We should get there in a half hour or so," he assured his friend as they headed north across the Golden Gate Bridge.

Two hours later, Tony began to grow concerned. Their car clung to the side of a mountain and there was no lake or port in sight. After three hours winding into California's interior, they finally turned onto Lakeport's Main Street, still uncertain if they'd arrived in the right place. Tony spotted someone on the sidewalk and rolled down the window.

"Hey, do you know where the Del Lago Clubhouse is?"

"Oh, are you guys here from Global Exchange to talk about Cuba?" the boy asked.

Tony was stunned. What were the chances that he would know that? The boy gave him directions, and they soon found the clubhouse a couple of miles down the road, on the water's edge. Marla greeted them at the front door, gushing and squealing. Before Tony could fit in a word, she grabbed his hand and dragged him around the packed room, making introductions. "This is my principal, this is the mailman, this is my basketball coach." It was obvious that they were there because of her charisma and enthusiasm.

The lights went down and Tony began his slide show. Members of the audience wore polite expressions as the images of Cuban children flashed onto the wall. Marla was sitting in front, her eyes shining.

Over time, Marla began to grow restless in Lakeport. She sought out a hands-on education in social justice activism with people who shared her beliefs. She skipped a week of classes to travel to Cuba with a peace group and volunteered at Global Exchange.

She began staying in San Francisco for longer periods, often over weekends, crashing with Medea Benjamin and her husband, Kevin Danaher, both Global Exchange cofounders. She quickly became an older sister of sorts to the couple's two daughters.

While Tony's visit and Marla's subsequent volunteering with Global Exchange officially initiated the teen into the grown-up world of activism, she continued to play the role of the all-American, California girl next door back in Lakeport. Her cotton-blond hair had darkened to a soft gold and her active lifestyle gave her an athletic, curvy figure. She and her brother, Mark, raced onto the lake in the family boat on lunch breaks to go wake-boarding. They sped along the town's streets in the protest-mobile, blaring music. She socialized with friends and partied on Friday and Saturday nights. But deep down, her heart wasn't completely in it.

In the spring of 1994, Marla signed up for a Global Exchange awareness-raising "reality tour" that would take her to the Mayan Indian villages and revolutionary communities of Central America.

In preparation for her trip to the first stop on the tour, Nicaragua, Marla pored over literature describing the stark social inequality in the country. She became intrigued by the country's revolutionary past. In 1979, the military wing of the Sandinista National Liberation Front, a leftist political party, toppled the decades-long corrupt and brutal dictatorship of Anastasio Somoza Debayle. With strong support from the poor masses, the Sandinista-led government junta instituted a number of leftist policies, such as land reform benefiting the peasant class and nationalization of private industry. By 1980, infighting ignited within the ruling junta, and the more moderate elements dropped out. In the newly elected Reagan administration, fear emerged that the government had designs for a communist state à la Fidel Castro's Cuba (which backed the Sandinistas). Remnants of Somoza's former National Guard, known as the Contras, were soon armed with controversial U.S. assistance and a vicious conflict ensued.

By the time Marla visited, the war was over. Nicaragua's first free elections were held in 1990, and with skyrocketing unemployment and inflation, the Sandinistas lost. Instead of repeating Nicaragua's pattern of bloody power shifts, the party peacefully stepped aside to make way for the new government.

Yet, the country had plummeted to the second poorest in the hemisphere. Swarms of children roamed the streets, and poor public sanitation had caused a cholera epidemic. To kick-start their trip, the Global Exchange reality tourists, or "delegates," visited with community representatives, labor leaders, and government officials in Managua, the country's crime-ridden capital. Following their crash course in the country's socioeconomic and political realities, the delegates boarded a bus and journeyed into the country's heartland.

Global Exchange's Michael Shellenberger led his small group to Estelí, a town in northern Nicaragua with strong Sandinista ties. Their local host had booked them into a grimy, run-down hotel. The American Global Exchange delegates bristled, looking on in horror. They requested that new arrangements be made, except for Marla, who wondered what everyone's problem was. "This is what's here, and this is what we'll take," she said.

The next stop on the tour, war-ravaged Guatemala, stirred her even more. Large numbers of the civilian population had been terrorized by the world's longest ongoing civil war at the time. In 1994, steps had been taken toward a peace agreement, but the war wouldn't officially end for another two years. Death squads aligned with the military brutally massacred indigenous Mayan civilians accused of supporting rebel factions. The delegates visited villages and local markets where peasant women hawked their goods. Marla marched right up to them, rummaging through her bag for money. Her tongue tripped out a garbled yet cheery, *"Hola! Cómo estás?"* Within moments, women were hovering around her. Withdrawing a wad of Guatemalan bills, she bought every trinket in sight and often intentionally overpaid.

During a visit to a Mayan women's cooperative where Marla was freely giving out money, Michael gently took her aside. "Look, you can't just go around giving out money. You're drawing too much attention. Plus it creates envy and jealousy in the community and strains the relationship between the gringos and the Mayans."

"But I want to help. How am I supposed to give a donation?" Marla asked.

"If you want to help, you can give money to an institution or an organization that will invest it better."

Marla listened and nodded. She apologized for her ignorance and promised to stop her compulsive giving. Breaking her vow, she continued handing out cash on the sly.

After a long day of meetings, the group sat down to a simple dinner in a local restaurant. Marla sheepishly asked Michael if she could drink a beer along with the older delegates. Michael agreed, as they weren't in America. She had a low tolerance and became woozy after two beers, but the next morning she sprang out of bed, ready to learn, notebook in hand.

In Guatemala, the group met with Witness for Peace, an organization that sent foreign volunteers whose mere presence in communities often deterred attacks by death squads. Marla was riveted by these speakers, taking notes furiously and asking questions.

The trip was life-altering, which she explained during a Lake County Community Radio interview in 1997:

> "I was a child during the whole Cold War scare, or whatever, and the horrendous things of the eighties were going on. When I was comparing myself to a girl my age in Guatemala, she was fleeing Guatemala and I was playing soccer. So you know, I was growing up in my beautiful childhood in this beautiful community and, you know, if you just look at the lake and the mountain long enough you can think, wow, there are no problems in this world. . . . I was getting things in the mail because I was doing research. When I read the first testimony of a woman who was raped and children were killed I was, like, calling every Guatemalan solidarity group and grassroots organization and saying send me literature now! And I was staying home from school reading,. Before I was doing anything I was reading, reading, reading, and I just couldn't believe that my whole life to think these things weren't going on and they really were going on.
>
> "After I went [to Central America], I saw, wow, me as an American citizen. I can use my middle-class background to get an education and further my activism. We organized an environmental club and I was the president of it or whatever, so I was, like, let's send a caravan [of relief supplies] to Guatemala and we did and I just started realizing, hey, let's start doing

things. And I can do things, I can get involved and really make a change and I'm going to study this."

Marla was also inspired by one figure much closer to home— her high-school English teacher, Laurie McGuire. Closely related to Marla's godmother, Eileen, Laurie watched Marla grow up.

Laurie employed an interdisciplinary approach to teaching and encouraged heated discussion about real-life sociopolitical issues of the day. During these discussions, Marla would eventually clamber onto her pulpit, expounding ideas and opinions, a performance which the other students relished.

In Laurie's senior year English class, one book struck a profound chord in Marla: *Cry, the Beloved Country*. Alan Paton's classic South African story unfolds after Arthur Jarvis, a white social reformer, is killed by a young black man during a robbery. The book explores the impact South Africa's racist apartheid policies had on society. Written in 1946, the book ends on a note of poignant, if wary, reconciliation between the aggrieved families of the killer and the killed.

After reading the book, Laurie's students examined the effects of apartheid, which led to decades of extreme poverty and disenfranchisement of the country's majority population. Inevitably the lesson's focus finally veered to Amy Biehl, a name most of the students were familiar with. The twenty-six-year-old blond Californian had been stoned, beaten, and stabbed to death by an angry mob in a South African black township in 1993, three days before she was due to return home. A Fulbright scholar, Amy was helping develop a voter registration program for blacks ahead of South Africa's first free elections in 1994. Like Paton's Arthur

Jarvis, she was killed by the very people she was trying to help. Her parents created a foundation in their daughter's name that provides educational and other programs for poor blacks living in the country's sprawling townships. Laurie said that Marla was incredibly moved, almost hypnotized, by the young woman's story.

"Go save the world, Marla!" the McGuire family cheered as their favorite little girl, all grown up now, burst onto the stage in her cap and gown. With diplomas in hand, the Clear Lake High Schools class of '95 was ready to celebrate. Rather than starting off her summer party-hopping with her classmates or going to Hawaii, Marla packed her bags for a trip to another island. She was going to Cuba on a protest tour with the Global Exchange–supported Freedom to Travel Campaign, in open violation of the U.S. travel ban.

Two classmates of Chelsea Clinton, the president's daughter, were breaking the stringent U.S. law along with Marla and forty other teenagers from across the nation. The year before, Chelsea's father had strengthened the thirty-three-year-old embargo on trade and the travel restrictions for academics, journalists, and Cuban Americans who had previously been allowed access to the country.

The risks involved with the trip were huge. A senior official in the U.S. Treasury Department sent participants a warning letter threatening ten years in prison and up to $250,000 in fines upon their return to the United States. Spending money in Cuba was against the law.

The students thought the embargo was a relic of the Cold War era that was now strangulating the Cuban people. Marla reasoned that restricting individual freedom of movement and prohibiting communication between citizens of two nations was a much greater crime than defying the travel ban.

On June 23, the group flew to Mexico City, where it boarded another plane destined for Havana. Marla decided to go all the way with the protest, confidently handing her U.S. passport over to be stamped when they arrived in Havana. Once in the capital, they hopped on rusty bicycles and spent the next week pedaling to health clinics, urban garden projects, schools, and youth groups. Marla also lounged on a powdery Caribbean beach and picked up some of her first salsa moves.

A week later, the teens walked up the Jetway at Houston Intercontinental Airport, ready to be handcuffed. Clad in T-shirts emblazoned with the Cuban flag, the young travelers hugged and cheered as they cleared U.S. customs.

"No law should keep us from going to another country. Someday young people like us will be working on policy, and we need to learn about other cultures," Marla told a *Houston Chronicle* reporter after she emerged from the plane, making it into a major U.S. newspaper for the first time. It wouldn't be the last.

Chapter 2

Global Exchange

(How to Excel in International Relations)

I left home to get a degree and to see the world. To my sur-
prise I found a scared young woman who was completely
in denial of who she was. This year my work wasn't that
great, but I found an amazing thing—myself! I do not have
all the answers, but I know that when I'm true to myself I
will be surrounded by beautiful, wonderful people. . . . I
have learned I can make it anywhere, and this was the
biggest doubt I had about myself and my work.
> —FROM MARLA'S ACADEMIC JOURNAL TO
> HER COLLEGE ADVISER, SPRING 1999

Southampton, New York, is better known for its
socialites than its social activists. It is, however, home to the
Friends World Program, boot camp for aspiring young do-
gooders. It is also nearly the farthest point from Lakeport on
the continental U.S. map. The tiny campus, which is
technically part of Long Island University, is incongruously

tucked among the mansions of the rich and famous. In the fall of 1995, Marla stomped into town.

Friends World offered the perfect training ground for Marla's grassroots, democratic aspirations. The alternative school is run by consensus, granting its small group of students nearly as much say in their education as the program's director. There are no grades, no final exams. Assigned reading is a rarity. Instead, students carve out their own curricula, with guidance from advisers, and keep an academic journal. At the end of each semester, they submit a "portfolio of learning." At the time, the program had campuses in Kenya, Costa Rica, Israel, and India, among other countries. It was just what Marla had dreamed of.

During her first semester in Southampton, Marla bonded with Christine Kozobarich who, like Marla, was an activist in high school. They had different characters and dispositions, but Marla was drawn to Christine's passion for Native American rights. On top of organizing rallies together, Christine and Marla, joined by Marla's roommate Erin, broke out of the insulated Friends World cocoon in Southampton to party with other Long Island University students.

In Southampton, the three girls met classmates Eduardo Moncada and Brett Rader, and the five became a tight clique. During their second semester of college, the five friends scattered around the United States for their first hands-on independent project. Marla gravitated to the nation's policy-making nexus, Washington, D.C. She landed an internship with the 50 Years Is Enough (50YIE) campaign, founded on the fiftieth anniversary of the creation of the World Bank and the International Monetary Fund. A coalition of more than two hundred nonprofit organizations dedicated to transforming the policies and practices of the international lending institutions, 50YIE demanded a number of reforms, including debt cancellation for poor nations and an end to supporting policies that promote "corporate globalization."

Marla did not walk through 50YIE's doors with the trepidation that most young interns possess. She barged into a conference room and interrupted a meeting.

"Hi! I'm Marla!" she said enthusiastically. "I'm the new intern here from Friends World, and I'm looking for a place to stay for a few months. Does anyone have space for me in their house?"

The audacity of the gesture disarmed her associates, one of whom offered Marla a spare bedroom in her apartment in nearby Chevy Chase, Maryland. It was a move the woman may have come to regret. Too focused on learning and networking to clean, Marla left her bedroom and much of the public space strewn with heaps of clothing and dirty dishes.

In September 1996, Marla grabbed her notebooks and pens, along with her bikini, and moved to Costa Rica for her first semester abroad. In comparison to its neighbors, the Central American paradise is a haven of security and prosperity. American surfers, snorkeling aficionados, and ecotourists flock to Costa Rica's beaches and canopied rain forests.

In the classroom, Marla and her friends spent long days learning about Central American politics, history, and culture.

They lived with local families and took a three-hour Spanish course daily. The group toured the region's poorer countries: Honduras, El Salvador, and for Marla, back to Nicaragua. The students met with various individuals and groups, from street children to political party leaders. Partly because Marla was a step ahead of her classmates in the region, and partly because she was Marla, she would often take the reins. She diverted the group to an impoverished barrio where they could talk with children, or to a church where a priest could impart an overview of a particular area. As they traveled down pocked dirt roads and through rural villages, Marla often led the young gringos in a sing-along or cheer.

Always on the hunt for an adventure, Marla and Christine, along with a few other friends, decided to take a side trip to get their scuba-diving certification. During their final dive, the group examined an underwater rock formation whose razor peak jutted above the water's surface. Lost in exploration, Marla got separated from Christine and the others. She finally surfaced—dangerously close to the jagged rocks. The heaving surf threw her against their sharp surface, lacerating her skin. She started to bleed.

"I'm okay! I'm okay!" Marla reassured her frantic friends as another wave tossed her into the rocks, her little body getting brutalized.

After returning to the capital upon the semester's close, Marla decided a party was in order. The previous academic year she had organized a "prom"-themed party, when all the students and staff from the Friends World global campuses gathered in Southampton. So, she thought, why not do the same in Costa Rica?

Marla rummaged through the thrift stores to find the perfect outfit. She had persuaded the staff of the group's favorite watering hole to host the bash. They had become fond of Marla and her friends and spray painted a large mural on the wall reading "Good-bye Gringos!"

December 31, 1976, Marla Ann Ruzicka ushered in the New Year with a cry to live. She weighed just three pounds, three ounces —half the size of her twin brother, Mark.

The emaciated infant was placed on life support. Hooked up to sterile tubes, she immediately began fighting for her life. A respirator rhythmically pumped oxygen into Marla's concave chest as she lay in the heated incubator.

Marla remained alone in the hospital for another three weeks, slowly gaining strength and building body mass. As Marla grew older her mother, Nancy, often told her daughter that she had learned a vital lesson in the womb: Women must work twice as hard to make space for themselves in this world.

Marla and Mark's early years had all the trappings of an idyllic childhood. Their father, Cliff, was a successful civil engineer and bestowed his new family with every comfort. The twins spent long summer days swimming in the lake, water-skiing and wake-boarding on its glassy surface in the early morning, and roaming in and out of friends' and neighbors' homes.

Although the twins were close as children, their personalities developed in starkly opposing directions. From the very beginning, Mark was introspective and quiet while Marla was hyperactive and intrepid. Marla approached strangers with guileless candor, as if she were born without the self-consciousness that inhibits most children. And she was fearless. No storm could prevent Marla from diving into the lake for a swim. She launched herself off dock rooftops without worrying if the water was too cold or shallow. Once, when the Ruzicka family was visiting Yosemite National Park when Mark and Marla were children, Marla jumped off a bridge without a second thought. Mark watched in horror as her body plunged into the boulder-strewn water below. To his relief, she surfaced, squealing with delight.

Marla commonly defended her brother when she thought he was being treated unjustly by a teacher. Marla would stand with her hands on her hips and scold the offender, unafraid of the repercussions. If he needed help, Marla was always the first to intervene.

Years later, when Marla was home from her sophomore year of college for winter break, Mark wasn't doing well. At nineteen years old, he had been diagnosed with bipolar disorder and was prone to spells of severe depression and destructive behavior, self-medicating with alcohol. His future was uncertain. Shortly after high school graduation, he worked on a land surveying project in southern California driving heavy equipment and testing soil. After three months, he enrolled at Humboldt State University in northern California to study environmental engineering, but he dropped out after one year.

Following his sister's lead, Mark would soon travel to Central America, where he enrolled in Spanish language classes in Guatemala. Marla thought village life might help Mark get onto a healthier track. Medea Benjamin of Global Exchange had a contact in the Honduran village of Lejamani, so she and Marla arranged for him to live there. Also like Marla, Mark was a humanitarian and organized a caravan of relief supplies that was sent to Honduras after Hurricane Mitch devastated the country in 1998. He began farming and, at first, things were looking up. But in the end, Mark's problems followed him to Honduras. He bounced back and forth between Lejamani and Lakeport and, at times, rehabilitation centers.

Marla tried to maintain her optimism by focusing her energies elsewhere. She gave presentations to Lakeport schoolchildren about Central America and social injustices, but Mark's battles were draining and they fought intensely.

In January 1997, she left for an internship in Havana. A journal entry in February reveals early feelings of depression—and her own roller coaster of wild ups and downs:

> "Well, 1997 has started off pretty tramatic [sic] but in a month I've already had numerous adventures. First question—why the fuck haven't I been keeping a journal? I'm quite a head case but it appears that I've survived the serious trials in mi vida. Southampton—the drive from SF to LIU was a quick, cigarette Snapple adventure to the scary world of my old life. Their [sic] are many people there who just don't get it. . . . I have so many lifes [sic] in different places I try to live them all as they just used to be. Boys hurt—Colby rocks. Mark will get better just as this fucking blockade will end. Man, here I am in

Cuba—I see a huge mansion crawling with children—
in the US would one of Trump's houses ever become
a school for poor children? I think not and that is why
I love it here. A country that takes care of its people.
I want to be a person who takes care of my loved ones.
Sometimes I feel that I failed Mark. Distance is tuff—
he bends all those who love him into a crazy frenzy. I
just have so much love I can't stay in just one place.
I'll never see the darkness like last week."

Marla ended up alone that semester, volunteering at a
Cuban state-run day-care center, helping out Global
Exchange when the reality tour delegations came through
town, and taking classes at the University of Havana. She
maintained regular contact with Medea Benjamin.

Medea arranged a home for Marla in Havana. She lived
with a feisty woman nicknamed Abuelita, Spanish for granny.
Medea had become fast friends with Abuelita and another
outgoing elderly woman during one of her Global Exchange
trips to Cuba. They loved Marla but were perplexed by her
gullibility and idiosyncrasies.

Not long after Marla arrived in Havana, she fell ill. Rather
than dwell on the loneliness of being hospitalized in a foreign
country, Marla culled inspiration from the experience.

Later, she loved to tell the story about the hospital—how
they didn't bill her. She thought, "If Cuba can have universal
health care, why can't we?"

Marla's junior year in college marked a continental
shift away from her devotion to the problems and politics
in her own backyard. While her passion for salsa dancing

and Che Guevara (the poster boy of Latin American revolution and social equity) would never fade, it was time to discover the rest of the world. Africa was as good a place as any to start.

Marla and her clique from Friends World—Erin, Christine, Eduardo, and Brett—all signed up for a semester in East Africa that began in Machakos, Kenya. Friends World had converted an old Peace Corps center on a coffee plantation into a small campus in the dusty region dotted with acacia trees.

The heat was unbearable. The young women were approached in threatening ways by a number of local men. Electricity came and went without warning. Classes, when they convened, were held in outdoor huts or the dining hall. There was one vehicle on the isolated plantation, and the only person who knew how to drive it spent most of his time in the local bar. While there, Christine struggled so severely with depression that she didn't think she would have survived the semester without Marla's constant encouragement.

The director of the program, a Kenyan who worked for the World Bank, had prepared "a safari semester" that included little in terms of education, according to Christine. In between Swahili language classes, the students often held "community meetings" to discuss ways they could enhance their Kenyan experience. Instead of simply whining about their situation, Marla conjured a temporary solution to the educational void: *She* would teach a class. Drawing on what she had learned while working for the 50 Years Is Enough campaign in

Washington, D.C., Marla improvised a class in the dining hall on World Bank reform.

Marla, Christine, and Erin, along with some other girls, shared a brick roundhouse with a concrete slab floor. They dubbed it the "bug house," because of the swarm of golf-ball-sized insects that lived alongside them. They drank water from a well. If they wanted warm showers, they had to build a fire to heat the water themselves. Unlike the other girls, Marla was always fine taking a cold bath. If someone had already built a fire, even better. She was incredibly flexible, a skill she had learned as a child when she was shuttled off to babysitters as her entrepreneurial mother was busy making deals.

One night, Marla bolted up in bed, awakened by a classmate's bloodcurdling scream. She flipped the sheet away from her body and the mosquito net over her head. In a flash, Marla was at the normally quiet girl's bedside.

"Oh my God, are you okay? Are you *okay*? What's going on?" Marla asked.

The other girls in the room squashed pillows over their heads to muffle the screams. They had grown weary of the regular midnight interruptions. The girl was taking Lariam, an antimalarial prophylactic that can cause nightmares and even psychosis. But time and again, Marla sprang up in bed, alarmed and concerned.

After quick stops throughout Kenya, the students crossed over the border into Tanzania. Their first stop was the northern town of Arusha, home of the International Criminal Tribunal for Rwanda, which was founded to prosecute the primary perpetrators of the 1994 genocide that claimed some eight hundred thousand lives. The group was anxious to sit in and observe the hearings, but the program directors had made sightseeing plans. They managed to witness some trials in intervals, making it hard to tell what was really going on. Marla was instrumental in voicing the students' collective dissent, lobbying their chaperones to change their itinerary as much as possible as the semester progressed.

The tail end of their East Africa studies took them to the predominantly Muslim island of Zanzibar, a short ferry ride off the Tanzanian coast. Marla and Christine stayed on for an extra week to relax. Like most young Western travelers visiting the island, they went for long swims in the Indian Ocean, smoked hashish, sunbathed, and dined on sumptuous seafood in between drumming lessons. Marla happily banged on her bongos each day, unconcerned with her inability to keep the rhythm.

Phillip Machingura first laid eyes on Marla at the Book Café in Harare, Zimbabwe. Despite its name, she wasn't poring over a book that hot African night in late December 1997. She was busy partying, soaking up a bit of local culture. Phillip intuited that Marla and her other Western friends were exchange students. He was right; the Americans were beginning the second semester of their junior year in Zimbabwe.

The twenty-one-year-old Zimbabwean worked double shifts at the downtown entertainment venue as an events booker and as a jazz singer for the band he managed, the Luck Street Blues. Marla caught Phillip's eye again a couple of nights later when she walked into the popular nightspot on the arm of Vincent, one of his bandmate's friends. Now he was definitely intrigued. The following Saturday night, a couple of days after New Year's, Marla and her friends charged into the Book Café and onto its dance floor. While Phillip was onstage crooning, he noticed that Vincent was absent. Although he felt slightly uncomfortable approaching an acquaintance's girl, he didn't forgo the opportunity to meet the gregarious blonde. As the band continued playing, he walked into the crowd to mingle. A bit shy and definitely cool, Phillip began to chat with a friend of Marla's. But the other girls guessed where his interests lay and announced that they were celebrating Marla's recent twenty-first birthday.

He introduced himself, and she gave him one of the Guatemalan friendship bracelets that she always kept in her purse. Marla pulled him onto the dance floor, where she kept the beat to a distant salsa tune that only she could hear between the notes of the sultry blues music. She gazed up at Phillip. His calm intelligent demeanor was uncannily familiar.

"You look just like my dad!" she chirped.

How was that possible, Phillip wondered, he being a black Zimbabwean of Shona descent, while Marla's ancestors clearly hailed from Europe?

Without any serious intentions, Marla and Phillip made plans to meet the following night at Harper's Night Club in a plush Harare suburb. She showed up with a friend and they all danced, the two friends drinking while Phillip abstained. They took a cab to the backpackers' lodge where the girls were living in town. Phillip and Marla talked into the wee hours of the night. Marla did most of the talking. She gushed openly about her favorite men, Lakeport, and college. By dawn, Phillip felt he already knew her family and friends.

Nothing proves the cliché that opposites attract more than the unlikely love affair that blossomed between them. She drank and he did not. She was excessively open with her feelings while he was protectively closed. He was black and African, she white and American. They were different in so many ways that Phillip often referred to their relationship as a "walking experiment," and their favorite lyrics soon became "You say tom-ay-to, I say tom-ah-to . . . let's call the whole thing off," which they often sang in unison. The terms and circumstances of the relationship were new to Phillip, as they were to Marla. It was his first serious relationship—almost too serious at the time, he said. Phillip and the Luck Street Blues played more than a hundred shows per year in towns all over Zimbabwe, and when he wasn't on the road, he was often busy rehearsing or working at the Book Café. His music was paramount, and he was determined to hit it big. But Marla was also determined to follow her heart and make the relationship work.

Marla continued with her studies while her love for Phillip grew. She was working on an "independent project." She took classes on feminism and political liberation taught by a well-known Zimbabwean professor and began exploring ideas for her senior thesis. Without a Friends World Center to guide her, or an internship to tame her, Marla's schedule was scattered and unfocused.

Fiercely committed to pursuing her own dreams—to somehow, some way improve the human condition—she needed to jump into the academic trenches for one last round. At the end of the semester, Marla left Zimbabwe and Africa uncertain whether she would ever see Phillip again.

Although Marla's head was momentarily in the clouds, she landed on her feet and hit the ground running in Israel her senior year. The semester in the Middle East was as intense as the conflict that surrounded them. Marla and her friends lived their first days in the Holy Land as many of its first Jewish citizens did: on a kibbutz, an Israeli collective farming community. They then moved to Jerusalem, where Marla shared a flat with five other students in the trendy Ben Yehuda Street neighborhood, bustling with shops, cafés, and international restaurants. The other girls dedicated time to personalizing their living quarters, securing shelves and pasting postcards to the walls. Marla hung a piece of cloth over her door and used her suitcase as a closet. Homemaking wasted valuable time.

Schoolwork was rigorous. Back-to-back classes exposed the group to the rich cultural, religious, and political histories—and contemporary realities—of both the Jewish and Palestinian populations. One Palestinian teacher lived in Bethlehem, located in the West Bank. She often had trouble passing through Israeli checkpoints leading into Jerusalem. Instead of missing the class on those days, students hopped on a bus and went to her for their lesson. Regular attendance was required. Marla and Christine relished the strict policy after their improvised schedule in Africa. Outside of the classroom, a hotbed of sociopolitical material awaited them on nearly every corner. No reading was required to understand that the Israeli-Palestinian conflict affected the daily lives of civilians on both sides of the dividing line.

The realities endured by average Palestinian families she met—many in the refugee camps of the territories and across the border in Jordan—disturbed Marla. The disturbance wasn't fleeting.

As in many places she visited, she didn't scratch much below the surface to inspect the region's complex historical and political context. In a way, it wasn't important to her. What was important was that the Palestinian children had little hope for a prosperous future. The roofs over some of their heads had been destroyed by Israeli bulldozers in antiterrorism raids. She often disappeared to attend protests against the demolitions on her own.

On one of their educational field trips, they met with a group that had recently started a new life in one of the controversial Jewish settlements. A resident who was originally from California talked about the grave security situation her family faced, even when visiting a shopping mall, where a suicide bomber could easily explode himself in a civilian crowd. Marla bolted out of her chair, seething.

"How can you complain? I don't want to hear about the safety of your children at the mall when you uprooted and came to a foreign place and occupied someone's homeland!"

While many of the students, such as Christine, might not have sympathized with the woman either, they bit their tongues.

Some fellow students were supportive of Israeli policies that Marla opposed. She could not tolerate a position she deemed corrupt and they often butted heads. Marla saw her own beliefs as morally right and had little patience for differing opinions. There was right, and then there was wrong. Marla's eyes discerned few shades of gray.

Marla also struggled with adapting to the culture of the region. The young men in the Friends World group often escorted the women home at night, which irritated Marla. If the girls weren't harassed by hormonal Israeli soldiers, then they were targeted by stone-throwing ultra-orthodox Jews offended by their exposed flesh. Shrugging off local custom, Marla lived her life as if she were in California, often wandering into the Arab markets braless in a tank top and shorts, smiling and greeting people as she shopped.

The walls were thin in the Ben Yahuda flat, betraying the extent to which Marla had succumbed to the frustration and emotional battles she faced in Jerusalem. Christine heard Marla cry herself to sleep on more than one occasion. Marla missed Phillip, despite many expensive late-night phone calls. Even though she was half a world away geographically—and a million miles away culturally—Lakeport was always present. Mark's problems persisted, and she struggled with being so far away from him, unable to help assuage his pain or temper his violent episodes.

The only place Marla could find respite was in exercise.

She joined the Ben Yehuda YMCA, where she swam dozens, and sometimes hundreds, of laps. But exercise was more than time to unwind; it was an obsession. Swimming, running, and Rollerblading were the only time she fully indulged herself—the only ways she could "be good to herself," she told friends. Her eating became spotty as well. Meals were often limited to munching on small cheese samples in bulk food stores, ostensibly for "the deal." She ate low-calorie frozen yogurt from a shop near their flat. At home, Christine noticed she barely touched food at all.

Despite Marla's hectic schedule, she found time to talk to Nancy on the phone several times a week. They often fought "like cats and dogs," according to friends, but also loved each other "to death." Their relationship was never broken, despite the fiery bickering. But the constant cheerleading for everyone around her pointed to a deep desire for a dose of approval for herself.

For her final semester, Marla rushed back into the warm embrace of Africa. Harare was just as she had left it, and so was Phillip. Soon after Marla arrived, the two young lovers moved in together. They were hardly ever in the small apartment. Phillip dedicated most of his time to his music, while Marla scrambled to collect research on her thesis. The topic of her final portfolio examined Cuba's national program training African doctors and teachers, with a focus on southern Africa. She had found a way to weave her two loves into one common subject.

They allotted time to meet for sandwiches at lunchtime,

and Marla attended nearly all of Phillip's performances. She drank too much, which bothered Phillip. It got so extreme at times that he refused to speak to her until she sobered up, leading to many arguments.

His conservative family wasn't accepting of her, and Phillip recalled a time when his elder brother looked upon the flip-flop-wearing blonde with disapproval. As always, Marla frequently spoke with her mother back in conservative Lakeport. Her family was similarly concerned about the relationship, warning Marla that Phillip might have several wives, which eventually became an inside joke between the couple.

She almost always joined Phillip on tour and took advantage of the trips to explore the Zimbabwean countryside. She forced him to take long hikes, which Phillip couldn't understand. It was so Western. Why walk for walking's sake? Marla also wanted a romantic holiday on the beach, and she was going to get one, despite her boyfriend's protests. Both of their bank accounts were low, and Phillip didn't have time for a break in his busy schedule. But Marla charmed their friend Jeremy Brickhill into lending them his beachfront property in neighboring Mozambique. The problem of transportation remained.

"I know, we'll hitchhike!" Marla declared.

Phillip was horrified, but he lost the battle. The Californian was determined to get out of the landlocked country for some quality swim time. They hit the road on what would be Phillip's first trip outside of his home country, their thumbs wagging in the air.

Once in Mozambique, they were picked up by a biracial family in an old Land Rover filled with people, fish, and prawns. They spoke only Portuguese, Mozambique's official language, and Marla somehow managed to communicate with them by speaking her own unique version of Spanish. The family dropped them off in the beach town of Vilanculos, and Phillip gazed upon the sea for the first time. Marla and Phillip went for long swims in the Indian Ocean. They spent a week gorging on fresh fish and lying on the deserted beach next to their palm-woven cottage. A photograph shows Phillip and Marla embracing playfully in the turquoise surf, their wide smiles iridescent in the sun.

But there were reminders of the world's ailments even in paradise. Scores of children, many with missing limbs, hobbled through Vilanculos. Mozambique's brutal civil war had ended in the early 1990s, but land mines remained for several years. They left their lasting mark on the country's most innocent citizens, and on Marla, who played and talked with them. She taught them a few English phrases and made them laugh and smile despite their condition.

Once back in Harare, Marla didn't stay still for long. She needed to refocus her energies on completing her thesis and went on an extended research trip to Johannesburg. Undeterred by the risk, Marla traveled back to Harare from the South African capital nearly every weekend to visit Phillip. Scraping by as usual, she boarded minibus taxis, and often at night, en route to Harare. At the time, a violent taxi turf war was raging in South Africa. Phillip was nervous about the dangerous journey.

As May approached, the inevitable grew near as well. Marla needed to return to the United States for graduation, and eventually, to find a job. Although she loved Phillip, she wanted to work for an American activist organization, which she saw as the route to changing U.S. policy. Zimbabwe was too far away from the people who could make a difference. They talked about seeing each other again, but their future as a couple looked bleak.

Marla's flight was leaving for New York. Phillip hugged and kissed at the departing gate. She promised to return soon for a visit. Phillip wasn't convinced, although he knew her intentions were sincere. The boarding announcement broke the mood. Bursting into tears, she kissed Phillip one last time and ran onto the plane.

Marla was the last of her small Friends World class to graduate during the informal ceremony. She sprang from her chair when her name was called, grinning from ear to ear. Her skin still golden from the African sun, she bounced across the short expanse of grass to accept her diploma. Marla thanked her parents, Erin and Christine, her "partner" Phillip, whom she loved and who couldn't be there, and Tony Newman, for first teaching her about Cuba.

Nancy and Cliff handed Marla a graduation present. When she opened the blue box, revealing diamond-and-pearl earrings, she became uncomfortable. Later, Marla vehemently demanded that her mother cash in the precious stones for a plane ticket to the United States for Phillip. When Nancy refused, Marla threw the box of pearls and diamonds at her. Nancy put them into her jewelry drawer, and that's where they stayed.

Chapter 3

Working Girl

(How to Protest for a Living)

I work for an organization where every day people call and
say I can't pay the electricity bill!
—MARLA PROTESTING AT SAN FRANCISCO'S COMMON-
WEALTH CLUB, JUNE 2001, AS SEEN IN THE DOCUMENTARY
ENRON:THE SMARTEST GUYS IN THE ROOM

Marla's first job was a disaster. The San
Francisco–based Rainforest Action Network (RAN), an
activist environmental organization, hired her as a development assistant in late 1999. RAN's grassroots ideals and
hands-on philosophy were a perfect match with Marla's own
beliefs, and she made a number of friends at RAN. The
administrative position they offered her, however, ended up
being a match made in hell.

Marla was eager to get started—and get her first pay-
check. She was crashing with Medea and her husband Kevin
Danaher of Global Exchange again, but now as a full-time

tenant. Their eldest daughter, Arlen, had left for college, so Marla moved into her bedroom, which overlooked Sanchez Street in San Francisco's Noe Valley neighborhood. She became a surrogate older sister to their youngest daughter, Maya. She rose early every morning full of energy and went jogging or Rollerblading up and down Noe Valley's steep hills before starting the day in RAN's downtown offices.

Medea noticed early on that Marla was gripped by sharp mood swings. She assumed they were simply a product of her youth. She cried easily and laughed hysterically. Run-ins with Mark were a constant source of tremendous stress and anxiety, exacerbating her emotional instability. Kevin, Medea, and their daughters became her second family, a much more liberal version of her own. Before long, Marla persuaded Medea and Kevin to accept another member into their family.

Marla and Phillip talked regularly on the telephone. She excitedly shared the news with him when she landed the job at RAN—but it meant she would not be returning to Zimbabwe. She suggested Phillip come for a visit.

Phillip didn't know how he would cover the exorbitant cost of a plane ticket from Harare to San Francisco. Marla offered to foot the bill. She was getting paid at RAN now, and she could borrow a little extra from Medea if she had to. But Phillip wasn't fond of the idea.

"I know!" Marla said, not taking no for an answer. "You can bring over one of those Shona sculptures. They sell really, really well here."

"Bullshit," Phillip said, knowing she was wheeling and dealing him.

In the end, she convinced him the plan would work. He could reimburse her for the plane fare once he sold his sculpture to one of the many high-paying African art connoisseurs in San Francisco. Having won the battle, she bought the ticket. Phillip arrived at San Francisco International Airport on a cold and sunny October day, his Shona sculpture tucked under his arm.

"We can give that to Medea!" was the first thing Marla told him when she greeted him at international arrivals, insisting it would make a perfect gift for their hostess.

Marla wanted Phillip to love her homeland, and although she had daily office work to tend to, she made time to introduce her boyfriend to as many friends and cultural experiences as possible. On Halloween, Marla dragged Phillip to the Castro district. Each October 31, San Francisco's vibrant gay and lesbian community and their friends let it all hang out, literally, in the streets. Men wearing leather chaps and not much else, or sequined dresses, strutted by. These were things that got men shot, or at least severely beaten, in the conservative Zimbabwean society. She drove him along the windswept California coastline; they hiked among the giant redwoods and walked along the beach at sunset. Back in San Francisco, Phillip indulged Marla in her favorite pastime: hunting for hidden treasures at yard sales. Marla was poor but content, and Phillip began to feel at home.

Marla was excited but nervous on the drive up to Lakeport. She desperately hoped that her family and friends would accept Phillip. Everyone would be there, gathered for Thanksgiving, and the plan was to hop from house to house to introduce him to the whole community.

In the end, nobody in Lakeport acted maliciously toward him, but he felt an undercurrent of discomfort and a level of naïveté inherent to small, insular towns the world over. Marla was aware of this and was concerned that her beloved Lakeport was ailing from a bout of provincial thinking. She wanted to change it, to fix it, to make it better. It was during this first visit to Lakeport that Phillip realized he and Marla were more alike than he had known. They both grew up in conservative surroundings, with conservative families. Although Phillip was raised in the city, he compared the soul of Lakeport to that of a Zimbabwean village.

While Phillip acclimated to the United States, Marla continued playing her miscast role in the office. Data entry was not Marla's strong suit. She was not detail oriented, and booking first-class plane tickets for her bosses annoyed her. Marla's boredom and irritation with the job turned into intolerance during the 1999 World Trade Organization meetings in Seattle.

A wide range of protesters streamed into Seattle and into the pouring rain from all around the globe to demonstrate for fair trade. An estimated fifty thousand to one hundred thousand people, from environmental groups and labor unions to farmers and students, clogged the streets and captured international headlines for several days during what was dubbed the "Battle in Seattle." Most of the protesters were relatively peaceable, but not all. More radical demonstrators attempted to sabotage the meetings. Blocking traffic at key Seattle intersections, they tried to prevent the world's trade ministers and other high-profile participants from reaching the convention center. One group calling themselves the "anarchists" led a violent campaign, vandalizing Seattle corporate property. Riot police sprayed rubber bullets and released clouds of tear gas into the crowds. Even RAN made the news by hanging a protest banner atop a crane. It was a protester's Super Bowl, the Olympics of social activism. The greatest international show on earth was unfolding a short plane ride away, and Marla was missing it. The development department was ordered to stay home, while everyone else at RAN got to go to Seattle. She was stuck filing in the office. Marla and her colleague Elizabeth Creely looked at each other, fuming.

"This is fucked up!" Elizabeth said.

"You're totally right. That's it. I'm never doing this again!" Marla huffed.

That weekend, Marla and Phillip jumped on a plane and, after landing in Seattle, hurried into town to meet up with her Global Exchange friends. The agenda had changed; the protesting was over. They were on clean-up duty. It was time to get the demonstrators out of jail.

The entire world seemed to be centered in Seattle that weekend, and they were at its core. Drenched to the bone, Phillip and Marla joined vigils for their imprisoned comrades. They sang "We Shall Overcome" as the cold December rain fell on their heads. They borrowed a friend's hotel room to wash up before rushing straight back into the wet streets for another round. Instead of scrambling to connect with her RAN colleagues, Marla helped Global Exchange pitch stories to the hordes of media looking for fresh news. Before long, RAN fired Marla.

Elizabeth was disgusted by the backhanded manner in which Marla was let go from RAN. Rather than being straightforward, she said, the development director demoted Marla, leaving her no choice but to pack up her desk and go. Storming out of a development meeting, Elizabeth packed up her own desk and quit in protest.

Elizabeth became one in a long line of older friends who felt excessively protective of the younger woman. Later Marla sought temporary refuge in Elizabeth's house on her trips back to San Francisco. She borrowed Elizabeth's clothes and forgot to return them. But she'd always arrive with her bags full of silk scarves she'd bought for friends in Thailand or Pakistan. Although thankful for the gifts, Elizabeth told Marla to save her money and look after herself instead, which she rarely attempted to do.

Marla married Phillip during her lunch break from her new post at Global Exchange on a blustery day in March 2000. Deciding to tie the knot that morning, they hadn't shopped for the occasion. Dressed in a simple gray sweater and black pants, her hair loose and uncombed, Marla ducked out of the offices and headed to city hall with Phillip. Two former colleagues from RAN stood witness. Snapshots of the ceremony show Marla holding a small bouquet of flowers as she kisses a rain-slickered Phillip. After getting hitched, they celebrated with Marla's closest childhood friend, Colby Smart, and his wife, Toni, Along with the happy couple, they did not spread the news to Lakeport.

Marla and Phillip decided it was time to get their own place and after a series of mishaps and bad luck with unseemly landlords, they settled into a cramped unit in a hillside house in Noe Valley, not far from Medea and Kevin.

Although her living situation was erratic, the one home Marla could rely on was Global Exchange, located next to a McDonald's restaurant in the heart of the Mission. After leaving RAN, she began working at the offices, which were strewn with protest banners and served fair-trade-approved coffee. At the time, Medea, who was well known as San Francisco's activist extraordinaire, was attempting to shift her public career from the nonprofit sphere to government. She joined the U.S. Senate race in 2000 as the Green Party candidate from California.

Tapping into the talent at Global Exchange, she hired Marla as campaign fund-raiser and the more meticulous June Brashares, an events coordinator at Global Exchange, as campaign manager. It would be the real beginning of Marla's long-awaited career.

Medea discovered that Marla was a born fund-raiser. Throwing pride by the wayside, Marla easily admitted to others that she didn't know enough and wanted to learn more. She sought out people she respected and hung on their every word. As if through osmosis, she soaked up their advice, which she quickly incorporated into her own fund-raising arsenal.

The three women traveled up and down the state throwing parties. The goal was to raise Green Party awareness and funds for Medea's campaign. Medea quickly identified Marla's strengths and utilized them. Marla could barely string a paragraph together and she was very scattered, but her skill at organizing people was very advanced for her age. Marla's hard work and knack for socializing paid off—literally. By the campaign's close, Marla helped raise $250,000. For the Green Party, this was a groundbreaking sum. According to Medea, only Green Party presidential candidate Ralph Nader had raised more.

Someone had brought a boom box, and Marla was leading the party, hopping around the station's lobby like a teenager at a school dance. *"Voulez-vous coucher avec moi ce soir?"* Marla beckoned the group of Green Party supporters who had crashed the debate at San Francisco's KRON television studios.

Earlier that day, one hundred fifty people had gathered in front of the building to protest the televised debate, from which Medea had been excluded. Without an invite, Medea, Marla, and June decided to organize a "debate" of their own out front. June said that they had a very difficult time getting coverage during the campaign and were forced to be creative, dropping in on editorial boards trying to drum up media interest. June later saw signs of these same tactics in Marla's own work in Afghanistan and Iraq.

Medea blamed the debate snub on Senator Dianne Feinstein, who, she said, blanketed the state with an expensive ad campaign but declined to engage in much public debate with her running mates. In response to what Medea deemed undemocratic practices, she and Kevin employed smear tactics against the longtime Democratic senator. They ran a radio spot that mockingly blamed the discovery of a new hole in the ozone layer on Feinstein's hair spray: "If you care about the environment, vote for Medea!"

Shortly before the election, Feinstein finally agreed to participate in two televised debates—but only with Republican candidate Tom Campbell. Medea struck an alliance of sorts with the Republican nominee, who had also been frustrated with Feinstein's silence, and they had debated each other on more than one occasion during the campaign. While both Republican and Democratic senators were debating California's ills under hot lights that late October day, Feinstein was the primary target of the Green Party's protest. At one point, Medea conferred with Marla and June and then turned to the crowd.

"Everybody stop! Listen up, there's been a new development. Dianne has just agreed to let me in and we can all go inside!"

It was a lie. But it worked. The protesters rushed by the perplexed police officers and flooded the building's lobby. Medea's plan was to storm into the studios for an instant, live debate, but they were locked out just in time. Her fib disclosed, the group decided to take advantage of their positioning and held an hours-long sit-in, or rather, dance-in. The press perked up, turning their lenses on Medea and Marla and the rest of the protesters. They'd finally gotten the media attention they coveted, becoming a hotter story than the debate itself.

On election day, Medea, Marla, and June were arrested. They interrupted a Democratic rally in San Francisco, yelling at Feinstein as she delivered a speech. Security dragged them away kicking and screaming. It was one of many brushes Marla would have with California law enforcement. It was routine; Medea, Marla, and their friends created a disturbance and resisted arrest before police officers whisked them away.

When the results of the election came in, Medea had garnered just three percent of the vote. Dianne Feinstein won the election by a landslide, but that didn't humble the Green trio. The women hopped on a plane to Florida, where they observed the presidential ballot recount in Palm Beach County. Staying with Medea's parents in the upscale beach community of Boca Raton, they hoped to fit in some vacation time on the side. It never happened. Instead, the three darted around the recount observation floor, NAACP hearings on the African-American vote, and a variety of press conferences. They were on their feet a lot, as they were not offered seats at the recount. Standing room only, they were told.

Taking their Green revolution from California to Florida, they lobbied the journalists covering the recount. "It's just rude," Marla told a reporter with the *Palm Beach Post*. Seats had been provided only for Democratic and Republican observers, although the move didn't appear to be an intentional rebuff. Nonetheless, Medea, Marla, and

June argued that the Green Party was just as legitimate as their dominant counterparts and should not be treated any differently. Instead of challenging the other observers, Marla broke the tension on the floor with her sparkly personality.

After George W. Bush won the presidential election, Marla and Medea traveled to Washington to protest his inauguration. Soon after arriving, they stumbled onto a gold mine. The two were walking near the Capitol when they noticed a group of people entering a large white house. Security guards blocked the front entrance. They suspected it was more than a housewarming party. Inquiring, their suspicions were confirmed. A reception was underway for the Florida delegation, and Katherine Harris, who was in charge of the recount that landed Bush in office, was the guest of honor.

"Oh, wow, Katherine Harris! I'm such a huge fan of hers. Can I go in and congratulate her?" Marla implored, charming the security guards with her girlish enthusiasm.

Assuming they were mother and daughter, the men agreed to let the harmless pair in. Marla bounced through the door.

"Hi, Ms. Harris, I'm Marla Ruzicka! I just want you to know that I'm a huge fan of yours, and, like, oh my God, I can't believe how the media treated you! I just want to tell you that you're a role model for young people like me," Marla gushed as Medea smiled sweetly by her side. "But I've got a really important question to ask you. How did you get away with stealing all those votes? I think it's *soooo* amazing that you got away with it! Everybody knows that Bush didn't win!"

According to Medea, Katherine Harris's jaw dropped when she realized what was transpiring. She made a beeline out the door, disappeared into an attending limo, and sped away. Soon after, a radiant Medea and Marla were tossed out.

Fighting the good fight on a full-time basis at Global Exchange, Marla achieved what she had always dreamed of. The focus of her fight, however, remained fuzzy. There was no single injustice she embraced. She was willing to put her gloves on for any worthy cause that would improve the human condition, whether it was campaigning against the sweatshops in Latin America or pushing big pharmaceuticals to lower prices for HIV/AIDS drugs in Africa. Then the lights went out, and everything became illuminated. The California energy crisis of 2001 provided Marla the opportunity to flourish as an activist.

The crisis was complicated and confusing. In short, the country's wealthiest piece of property, its Golden State, couldn't pay the bills. Behemoth energy companies—the now defunct and disgraced Enron Corporation being the most famous—took advantage of loopholes in the state's haphazardly deregulated energy industry. Companies starved the state of power until prices skyrocketed, leading to a series of rolling blackouts and plunging California into a state of emergency. To turn the lights back on, public utility companies were forced to pay the energy companies' astronomical fees, which were passed on to consumers. Companies like Enron purportedly made millions of dollars, while millions of Californians roasted in the summer heat, struggling or unable to pay their energy bills. Government indecision on the state and federal levels didn't ameliorate the situation.

Like the Israeli-Palestinian conflict, Marla didn't fully grasp the minutiae of the energy crisis. What she did understand, however, was that average Californians, and especially the poorer sections of the population, were wrongly suffering.

Throughout the Florida recount and the California energy crisis, Marla learned how to work the news media. She thought journalists were just plain, good fun. "They're the most interesting people in the world," she once said. Marla's Global Exchange contacts from her high school days, Tony Newman and Michael Shellenberger, had since left the organization and founded their own socially conscious public relations firm. She kept in touch with Tony on a fairly regular basis, seeking media relations advice.

Medea, Marla, and June went to work, organizing an outrageous campaign that once again took them from California's northernmost reaches to the Mexican border. They staged several "people's takeovers" of the state's power plants and stalked public utility, government, and energy company meetings, waving a wide array of clever protest banners. One of their favorites was "Stop FERC-ing California!"—playing on the initials of the Federal Energy Regulatory Commission. Medea and Marla turned their protests into themed costume parties to liven up the staid meetings—and grab headlines. They developed a symbiotic relationship and mentor soon began looking to protégée for inspiration.

During one brainstorming session, Marla came up with an idea that was sure to make for an interesting photo opportunity at the next energy meeting. Wearing goggles and coveralls to an energy meeting, like the three characters in the film *Ghostbusters*, the women bellowed, "Who do you call? Ratebusters!" When then-governor Gray Davis met with the energy companies, the protestors often wore pig masks, and with the help of her brother, Mark, even bought a live pig for emphasis. On one occasion, the squealing mascot relieved itself in the hallway outside of the governor's office. State troopers surrounded the feces, unsure of what to do with the evidence. The women were hauled out of so many energy meetings so many times that they were on a first-name basis with the state troopers.

In the end, their antagonistic tactics seem to have made a dent in the state's consciousness. Medea said they really "put the screws" to the California governor and took credit for stirring up a lot of the anti-Davis sentiment during the energy crisis. In the years that followed, his popularity continued to plummet. In 2003, a gubernatorial recall election was ordered by referendum. Arnold Schwarzenegger won.

At the peak of the crisis, the Global Exchange girls started a campaign urging Californians to ignore their energy bills and even stoked a "burning of the bills" bonfire in front of a public utility meeting. Thinking creatively, they bought energy company stock to gain access to shareholder meetings, where they would surprise the attendants with a pithy protest slogan. The documentary *Enron: The Smartest Guys in the Room* includes a shot of Marla screaming, "I work for an organization where every day people call and say, 'I can't pay the electricity bill!'" as two security guards hold her back.

Marla's most momentous publicity coup of the energy crisis took place when President George W. Bush was attending a fund-raising luncheon at the Beverly Hills Hotel during the height of the crisis. A friend of Medea's with connections in Los Angeles managed to scrounge up a few tickets to the private function. Security at the event would be airtight, requiring Medea and Marla to be even more inventive than usual.

As President Bush presided over his guests, Marla stood up and ripped off her sarong. She lifted it up over her head, spreading her arms wide. The skirt was actually a protest banner with a slogan printed on its underside: "Stop the Energy Rip-Off!" Marla was swarmed by security and led away.

Marla's career had taken off and Phillip's had too, but not exactly as he planned. The pursuit of musical stardom was put on hold.

His first dip into activism took place at Global Exchange. Marla roped him into working on Medea's campaign. Phillip even attended a weeklong activist training camp, and he and Marla attended talks given by Kim Klein, a grassroots fundraiser. Marla believed that raising money from everyday people, rather than large foundations, simultaneously raises public awareness.

While Marla spent more and more time on the road during the campaign and California energy crisis, Phillip worked on developing his skills. He went to New York City in the fall of 2000 for an internship working with a welfare-rights activist group. Upon his return to San Francisco, he was hired by the organization, whose headquarters are located across the bay in Oakland.

In June 2001, Marla and Phillip managed to briefly synchronize their schedules. They were both passionate about finding ways to fight the HIV/AIDS pandemic, which was ravaging Zimbabwe and other African countries. Taking a breather from the energy crisis, Marla traveled with Phillip to New York for the United Nations General Assembly's special session on HIV/AIDS.

Marla called a friend at a radio station, who doctored some fake press credentials so they could get in. Once there, they hooked up with friends at Health Gap, an umbrella group of nongovernmental organizations advocating for universal access to HIV/AIDS treatment. When representatives from Muslim countries boycotted a speech by a conference delegate who worked for a gay and lesbian organization, Marla helped organize a protest of the boycott within the building. Marla and Phillip were kicked out and threatened with a lifetime ban from the UN headquarters.

Shortly after their trip to New York, Phillip and Marla began seeing other people. Despite sharing similar passions, their lives were drifting apart.

They stayed close friends, and Phillip had difficulty explaining the nature of his relationship with Marla to his new girlfriends, causing him a fair amount of grief. She remained the most important woman in his life even when their lives started taking different tracks.

Marla was still ricocheting from one social cause to the next in 2001 when a warm September day finally gave her a direction.

War on Terror 101

(How to Find Civilian Casualties in a War Zone)

It's a terrible tragedy. We are against any more innocent victims being taken.
— MARLA AT THE FUNERAL OF AN ARAB-AMERICAN
SHOPKEEPER KILLED IN A HATE CRIME,
OCTOBER 2001, ASSOCIATED PRESS

Marla was in an unusually good mood the morning of September 11, 2001. She'd organized a successful HIV/AIDS fund-raiser the night before and things were looking up. She bought some bagels at a local bakery for Medea and her coworkers in celebration, then jumped into the protest-mobile for the short commute to work.

Driving through Noe Valley toward the office in the Mission, she switched on the radio and flipped the dial to KFOG, her favorite rock station. There was no music. Instead, a distressed voice crackled over the airwaves.

Nobody knew how many people had perished in the infernos from the terrorist attacks, but the figures were well into the thousands, horrifying Marla along with the rest of the world. Mothers and fathers, daughters and sons, husbands and wives had gone to work that day, never to return.

The only certainty in those early hours was that, in one terrifying instant, the course of history had taken a sharp and devastating turn. Marla didn't know it yet, but her own destiny had also been irrevocably changed.

She accelerated down the hill, parked, and ran into the Global Exchange offices on the corner of Mission and 16th Streets. Immediately after hearing the news, Phillip sped from Oakland over the San Francisco Bay Bridge to be with her. They comforted each other, but there wasn't much time to grieve—she had too much to do. Her workload had just expanded beyond the limits of her imagination.

Global Exchange organized a vigil and a concert starring the lead singer of the rock band Spearhead, both in support of the September 11 victims and to rally against hate crimes. Some one thousand people attended the concert in the Mission's Precita Park, where Marla didn't stop moving in an organizing frenzy. She knew every journalist there and was busy pitching stories and arranging instant interviews.

In late September Marla joined a slumber party in the Mission District's City Blend Café. Its Iranian-American owner had received threatening phone calls, and someone had smashed his shop windows. To express solidarity and spread a public message of tolerance, Marla and her companions lugged their sleeping bags to City Blend and camped out for the night. She also attended the funeral of an Arab-American man who had been gunned down in front of his rural California convenience store by unknown assailants in a possible act of misguided reprisal for the terrorist attacks. Most of all, she began spending time in Fremont.

Located in the suburban sprawl east of San Francisco, Fremont is the Afghan capital of the United States. Some seventy thousand Afghan immigrants reside there and in the surrounding communities. After September 11, Fremont grew tense. Rocks and bottles were thrown in front of at least one of the town's many Afghan restaurants. Fremont's Afghans were worried about their friends and family back home. The backlash that would hit Afghanistan was sure to be much stronger.

Medea and Marla went to a restaurant in Fremont to meet with ordinary Afghans. After talking to some of the diners, they were referred to a local women's group. Together they organized a speaking event at Hayward Community College promoting peace; it featured prominent women such as author Alice Walker and attracted some one thousand people. Planning the event, however, was cluttered with unexpected complications. Widely diverging interpretations of Islam surfaced, and the women squabbled. Political opinions varied as well. Medea bristled. Not everybody in the Afghan community was against the war. On the contrary; many Afghans supported the American-led bombing campaign, which they hoped would rid their homeland of the hated Taliban—despite the danger it posed to ordinary families caught in the crossfire on the ground. Marla had a steep learning curve.

Medea and Marla sat glued to their television screens at night as the bombing campaign in Afghanistan was under way. Precision-guided missles prevented unwanted civilian deaths, the pundits and military spokesmen said. But Medea knew that civilians must be dying, no matter how sophisticated the weaponry. Antiwar activists and military brass alike would agree: Some human collateral damage during war is a given, even when care is taken to avoid civilian death or injury. Mistakes are inevitable.

Medea decided to up the ante; they would find out for themselves. She assembled a female-only fact-finding delegation that would travel to Peshawar, Pakistan, and on to Afghanistan. One of their new Afghan women friends was supposed to serve as guide and cultural ambassador, but at the last minute, she dropped out. The remaining four—Medea, her twenty-one-year-old daughter, Arlen, Global Exchange colleague Deborah James, and Marla—decided to go anyway. To avoid any extra stress, Marla initially told her family she was going to London. She called Nancy the night before her flight with the truth. However, she let Phillip know about her plans well in advance. He implored her not to go, but she wouldn't listen.

June drove her colleagues to San Francisco International Airport a week before Thanksgiving. They were nervous but maintained a positive tone—their mandate was a crucial one. A journalist showed up at the airport for the send-off, and Marla brimmed with excitement as she passed through security. She had spent her whole life preparing for a human rights mission of this magnitude. It was just a twenty-four-hour plane ride away.

Hordes of journalists roamed Peshawar in search of news. They didn't have to look far. Refugee camps teemed with new arrivals fleeing the bombing in Afghanistan, and thousands of anti-America rioters clogged its dusty streets. But by mid-November the media had grown bored with the story. The main attraction was next door, just over Pakistan's western border.

By late November, the U.S. bombers, aided by American Special Forces and Afghan militiamen on the ground, had chased the Taliban from power. The Taliban had fled the nation's battered capital, Kabul, retreating to their base in Kandahar in the country's south. The remaining cadres would soon abandon Kandahar as well, melting into the country's stark and mountainous backdrop. Journalists scurried to find rides to Kabul. They wanted to witness history, imagining Afghans tossing their turbans and burkas aside to celebrate in Kabul's cratered streets. They camped out in smoky Pakistani offices, desperate to win a coveted exit visa, and thronged the border in packs.

The Global Exchange delegation arrived in Peshawar with little more than determination. They found a guest-house on the side of the road, checked in, dropped off their bags, and started knocking on doors. A nongovernmental organization, known as an NGO, guided them into the congested refugee camps, where they hoped to find proof that civilians were dying in Afghanistan.

Afghans had been fleeing violence at home long before

September 11, 2001. At that time, there were already two million Afghan refugees living in Pakistan. A majority of the Afghan refugees living in these squalid, makeshift communities had depended on the United Nations and other charities for food and shelter for years. Decades of conflict, from the Soviet invasion to a subsequent bloody civil war culminating in Taliban control, had ripped Afghanistan apart at the seams, reducing buildings to rubble and tearing human lives to shreds. In the weeks leading up to the U.S. bombing campaign, experts predicted that up to one million new Afghans could arrive. The number ended up being much lower. Nonetheless, there were tens of thousands of new residents in Pakistan. Some ran to safety before the U.S. bombs hit; others fled after, carrying nothing more than stories of personal tragedy. Unable to gain quick access to Afghanistan, the Global Exchange delegation found the camps and the international aid agencies in Peshawar to be fertile ground for their research on civilian casualties and suffering caused by Operation Enduring Freedom.

There were so many new Afghan refugees in and around Peshawar, the women needed only to set foot outside of their guesthouse to find the tales of devastation they were hunting for. Medea remembers stumbling on a thirteen-year-old Afghan girl begging in the street. Her house was accidentally hit by bombs and her mother was killed. Her father was so distraught he became mute. The girl became the head of the household, taking care of her father and a younger brother and sister. She had to figure out how to get the family out of the country and into Pakistan.

Marla was deeply affected by the refugees' stories, and the mission quickly became much more than official business to her. She bought medicine for sick refugees and tried to help individual families in any way she could, giving them food or money, or simply a hug. There was only so much help Marla could offer with compassion and what little pocket change she had.

There was one thing she could do. The best way to help these desperate families was to tell their stories to the world. Marla knew from her media work in California that the only way to do that was to get to know the journalists.

Marla persuaded a team of MSNBC television journalists to accompany them to the camps. Medea said that the delegation itself became the unintended focus of the network's story. As Medea spoke seriously into the camera, Marla played with a group of Afghan children in the background, teaching them how to say "I love you!"

The San Francisco women listened wide-eyed to one tragic story after another. The three younger delegates had never brushed so close to war before and were shocked by its consequences. A mother told of a day in the park with her children when a bomb meant for the nearby Kabul Airport landed in the playground instead. Three children were killed. Another woman was crushed by a U.S. food package that fell from the sky and crashed through her roof. A child was blown up when another aid drop detonated a land mine.

Meanwhile, Medea assigned Marla and Deborah to visa duty for entry into Afghanistan. They eagerly passed by the Pakistani offices three days in a row. The visa officials' enthusiasm did not match theirs. Posing as journalists with phony press credentials doctored by Kevin, the two young women flashed sweet smiles in vain. The listless men glanced at them wearily. Cigarettes dangled from the corners of their mouths. It was time for lunch. Would the ladies please return tomorrow?

While they waited to be issued visas, news reached Peshawar that armed men in turbans had ambushed a convoy of journalists traveling on a desolate stretch of road that connects the Afghan city of Jalalabad to Kabul. Four reporters, an Australian, a Spaniard, an Italian, and an Afghan working for a British news agency, were stoned and shot dead on November 19. The tragic event cast a dark cloud over Peshawar. The murders seriously spooked Medea's daughter Arlen. Besides, the delegation needed to prepare for a December 6 press conference in Washington, D.C., where they would report their findings. Medea reasoned that the delegation had collected enough data in the Pakistani refugee camps to present an accurate snapshot of the realities on the ground in Afghanistan. The second phase of their mission was aborted.

Marla and Deborah, however, decided to pay their cigarette-smoking friends one last visit. Four times was the charm. To their surprise, the clerks issued their visas. A group of journalists was leaving in an hour and a half. All they needed to do was show up to join the convoy, which was traveling under the protection of Haji Qadeer's militiamen. The warlord from Jalalabad had been living in exile for six years. After the Taliban disintegrated, he wrested back control of his hometown and was Jalalabad's new governor. Bandits and other armed groups continued to roam the anarchic territory, and the armed guides were welcomed.

The two women rushed back to the guesthouse, packed their bags, and said their good-byes to Arlen and Medea, who were returning to San Francisco. Marla and Deborah promised they'd be back in San Francisco with enough lead time to help out with the press conference in Washington, D.C. And then they were gone.

Marla had very little cash left. But she gladly paid Haji Qadeer's men the cost of the trip into Afghanistan. The hundred-dollar fee was the best career investment of her life. The stories they'd heard from the Afghan refugees in Pakistan were compelling and, if true, devastating. But Marla wanted to see the hard evidence with her own eyes.

They climbed into an SUV and met their travel companions: a Russian journalist who had taken part in the Soviet invasion of Afghanistan in his earlier days; several British reporters; and Haji Qadeer's son and nephew. The engines revved and turned west toward Afghanistan for the bumpy journey. They swept onto the Khyber Pass, slicing through the jagged Hindu Kush mountain range. Some seven hours later, they rolled into Jalalabad.

Deborah and Marla remained under Haji Qadeer's care and were dropped off at the family-owned guesthouse. It wasn't luxurious, but it was well-looked after, clean, and intimate. With its small courtyard, six rooms, and a kitchen where staff cooked their meals, it felt a little bit like home. They dined on the floor, as was Afghan custom, and discovered their first local delicacy, the pomegranate fruit.

The Taliban forces and al-Qaeda had left Jalalabad, heading toward the White Mountains to the south, where Osama bin Laden had once lived. They left belongings behind in their hasty departure. Journalists found houses filled with uniforms, weapons, and Arabic military manuals illustrating in precise detail how to kill a human target. These abandoned souvenirs served as reminders of the lethal threat that the regime and al-Qaeda had posed.

The morning after arriving, Marla and Deborah bundled up against the cold and headed out into the surrounding area with a translator to assess the damage the United States had caused in its campaign. Serrated mountain peaks slashed the horizon. A polar wind whipped up a fine layer of dirt, which burrowed into the corners of their eyes, their nostrils, their ears. It was unthinkable that crops had ever grown in this stark land.

They came upon a two-hundred-foot crater in the ground and were told that it had once been an al-Qaeda military camp. They drove on, passing rusted skeletons of tanks, evidence of decades of war. Then they encountered an agonizing by-product of the most recent one.

Rows upon rows of brittle structures lay out before them. They were the new homes for countless Afghan "displaced persons" who hadn't made it across the border to Pakistan before and during the bombing. The hungry, cold families who had fled their villages had patched together the shabby tents, nothing more than a few pieces of old cloth and food-aid sacks from international aid agencies supported by sticks. There were no bathrooms, no signs of running water. Marla and Deborah also visited more orderly displaced camps that aid agencies had managed to reach. They watched children play in a village outside of Jalalabad despite the harsh circumstances. Their hair was tinged orange, a symptom of malnutrition. Marla talked to displaced families and villagers, transferring stories of war and hunger into her notebook.

Jon Swain had had a long day. In his fifties, fit for his age, he had a lithe frame and full head of salt-and-pepper hair. Soft-spoken, there was a certain air of melancholy about him. His eyes were large and pale. Like Marla, the veteran war correnspondent had come in from Peshawar with Haji Qadeer's men and was staying in the governor's guesthouse. John had stories to file at the end of each week for London's *Sunday Times* newspaper, so like every journalist, he scampered to lay claim to an empty room that he wouldn't have to share with any of his colleagues. To his joy, he was successful. After briefly unwinding, Jon decided to take a look around. There were glass panes on the doors, and as he walked past the adjacent room, he noticed three women sitting on cushions spread out on the floor, sipping tea and eating pomegranates. He went in to say hello.

"Hi, I'm Marla!" she greeted him with a smile as he entered.

Marla noticed that Jon looked very tired. She was concerned about the stranger's well-being and was seemingly oblivious to Afghan social decorum.

"Oh, you look really stressed out. You need to relax!" she trilled.

Before he knew it, Marla had turned the reserved Englishman flat on his tummy. Straddling him, she began drumming on his back, giving him an expert massage. He was shocked.

He looked up and several Afghan faces were peering through the glass door with a look of curiosity and envy.

She ground the knots out of his shoulders, and they chatted for a while, munching on pomegranate seeds. Marla told him she was planning to travel to Kabul the next day.

After a few days in Jalalabad, the women had been offered security from Haji Qadeer to travel to Kabul. The mayor was going anyway, and they were welcome to join the convoy. They were apprehensive. It was the same road the four journalists had been killed on just a week earlier. Medea and Deborah were actually due back in San Francisco with their important documentation, which Medea needed for the press conference in the capital. Their report, after all, was the purpose of the delegation's visit to the region. Marla tossed her fears and press conference responsibilities aside. She wanted to gather more critical information. She had gotten this far and wanted to push on.

Angered, Deborah made her way back to Peshawar and onward to San Francisco alone. Marla, meanwhile, arrived in Kabul in one piece. She was ecstatic, taking in the dramatic scenery on the final stretch of road that descends into the valley that holds Kabul. She was only in Kabul for a couple of days, tagging along with journalists and trying to learn as much as she could about the city and the humanitarian situation in the country. Kabul had been hit during the U.S. bombing, but most of the raids took place in rural areas. Afghanistan's previous wars, however, had chipped away at Kabul's structures for years and were responsible for most of the city's destruction.

The Taliban had not been gone for long, and all was chaos. Elation and fear mingled in the chilly air. The Northern Alliance militias clutched their weapons as they patrolled town. Only the bravest of women removed their burkas in public. Journalists and aid workers arrived in droves from Pakistan and camped out in electricity-free hotels and compounds. Everyone was eager to discover the new Kabul. It had literally changed overnight.

In early December, B-52 bombers unleashed a fierce attack on Tora Bora, a manmade cave complex in the mountains near Jalalabad where the United States suspected Osama bin Laden and his foot soldiers were hiding. The bombs not only pummeled their intended targets; they also flattened some neighboring villages. News of the raids trickled into Kabul. Civilians had been killed, and the injured were pouring into Jalalabad's main hospital. Latching onto her new journalist friends, Marla made a U-turn.

World War II had taught the international community a painful lesson. Some thirty-seven million civilians, from Japan and China to Russia and Germany, were killed. Everyone had blood on their hands, if some more than others. As a result, international law was drawn up calling for the protection of noncombatants—unarmed men, women, and children—in times of war. The Geneva Conventions of 1949, and their subsequent amendments, spell out the legal obligation of warring factions to do as much as possible to respect the rights and lives of civilians during any form of conflict, whether international or domestic in nature.

Despite the world's recognition of the importance of protecting civilians during war, statistics are alarming in the new millennium. During World War I, some 95 percent of those reported killed were combatants. Today, the statistic is inverted. Soldiers' lives are still tragically lost, but 95 percent of people killed in the dozens of wars raging around the world are civilians.

The Vietnam War cost the military enormous troop losses—and the nation's trust. Since that time, the United States has largely shifted the initial stages of its wars from the ground to the air in order to minimize the number of soldiers killed. Aided by advanced technology, the United States also attempts to avoid massive civilian casualties by using precision-guided missiles and bombs. When possible, the Pentagon carefully gauges the civilian cost of a military hit before striking. The importance of the target is weighed against the number of people who might die in an attack. There is usually a "magic number," which falls somewhere between a handful of civilians and a few dozen. Sometimes military personnel receive faulty intelligence about a particular target, or a human error is made. In other cases, some "collateral damage" is deemed unavoidable when bombing a threatening target located in a civilian area.

Determining the number of civilian casualties in a conflict as complex as Afghanistan's can prove impossible. The truth is often lost in a haze of violence and confusion—the "fog of war." Despite precautions taken to minimize civilian harm in Afghanistan, it was estimated that as many as two thousand ordinary people, most of whom probably despised the Taliban and hadn't even heard of Osama bin Laden, were killed. Many of Afghanistan's rural areas are impossible or very difficult to reach by land—especially in December as the winter snows arrive. Bodies were buried quickly, as is Muslim custom. With the war raging on, most villages were located in areas that were simply too dangerous to visit. One intrepid aid agency said it removed seventy-two bodies from a bombed village. Afghan groups with differing allegiances and agendas made various claims about the number of dead around Tora Bora. Each reported figure was just a drop in an increasingly murky bucket of quantification. Nobody was responsible for tabulating the dead. All anybody knew for certain was that scores, perhaps hundreds or even thousands, of civilians had been killed.

Marla mustered the courage to visit the Jalalabad hospital several times to conduct her research. She stared in horror at the men, women, and children stretched out in agony on bloodied sheets and began crying hysterically behind her veil, which she finally conceded to wearing. Some were missing arms and legs. Scraps of sharp mortar had wounded others, lacerating their skin and puncturing their organs. Bodies were piling up in the morgue. It was mayhem.

Meanwhile, Medea, Deborah, and Arlen appeared on December 6 at the National Press Club in Washington, D.C. The delegation called for an international peacekeeping force to help deliver food assistance to hundreds of thousands of Afghans. The anarchy of war had left aid agencies vulnerable to roaming armed bandits. They also demanded a halt to the U.S. bombings in order to stem the flow of refugees, an investigation of civilian casualties, and a major U.S. financial commitment to rebuilding Afghanistan. They warned that refugees were dying from cold and hunger, and that graveyards were springing up next to camps. In short, their message was that America needed to take responsibility for the mess its war had made, regardless of the horror of September 11. According to Medea, very few American outlets covered the story.

With the press conference under way in Washington D.C., Marla was busy making her own American media contacts. She wanted to sniff out the foreign press corps in Jalalabad, so she crashed a dinner at the Spinghar Hotel, where most journalists were staying.

In early December 2001, Pam Constable of the *Washington Post* was staying at the Spinghar—which means "White Mountain." While most journalists had "parachuted" in from other parts of the world to report on the war, Pam was an old hand in the region. Based in neighboring Pakistan, she had covered news in Afghanistan throughout Taliban control of the country and had stayed at the Spinghar many times. The ramshackle, colonial hotel had seen better days. Before September 11, it was dark, freezing cold, and almost always empty. After, it was dark, freezing cold, and crowded five to a room. The mountain temperatures dropped so low at night that the journalists slept with all their clothes on.

The mood was somber at the Spinghar, despite the adrenaline rush of covering the war. Many guests knew the four journalists who had been killed on the road to Kabul. Some of them actually had been in the convoy. Pam was one of them. To cheer themselves up, they dined together most evenings and created a Thanksgiving feast. One evening, Marla bounced up to their table as if she'd gotten lost on the way to a slumber party. She was wearing pajamas with cartoon animals under an Afghan robe.

"Hi everyone! I'm Marla!" She waved to the journalists with a goofy smile. "I've just arrived in Jalalabad and I'm here with Global Exchange checking out the human rights situation caused by the war."

The journalists shot one another puzzled glances over their coffee cups. Marla left them stunned. It was because of such encounters that Marla earned the nickname "Bubbles."

Back at the Haji Qadeer's guest house, Jon Swain and Marla talked for hours during those days in early December. The conversations marked a critical turning point in Marla's life.

Marla joined Jon on reporting assignments and was exposed to the human cost of war, which was his journalistic focus. Back in the guesthouse at night, she told him about Zimbabwe, and they discovered that they had a few things in common. He had also spent some time there and knew the Book Café where she had met Phillip.

He told her about the dangerous and violent stories he had covered in East Timor, Kosovo, Republic of the Congo, Rwanda, Bosnia, Beirut, Cambodia, and Vietnam. He was portrayed by actor Julian Sands in the classic Cambodian war film, *The Killing Fields* and had once been held hostage for several months by rebels in Ethiopia. Over the years, Jon had lost many friends and colleagues to war. On several occasions he barely escaped with his own life, surviving only because of the intervention of local friends, the color of his skin, or pure luck.

Marla was mesmerized by the compassionate edge to Jon's storytelling and clung to his every word. Like she did with other seasoned figures in her life, Marla looked to Jon for guidance and inspiration. She knew a valuable mentor when she saw one.

She told him about her own work in Afghanistan and that she wanted to do something to make a difference. They talked about the war victims she'd seen in the hospital and the families that had been killed in villages like Kama Ado, where one hundred fifteen civilians had been killed by a one thousand pound bomb.

Overcome with emotion by Jon's own experiences and the scale of tragedy she'd witnessed, Marla had an epiphany: She would find a real way to help civilian war victims in Afghanistan. If she was daunted by the nearly impossible task, she didn't show it.

Before Jon left Afghanistan for the Christmas holiday, he gave Marla a copy of his book *River of Time*, addressing it "To my Tora Bora Princess." Marla came to treasure the book.

Not long after Jon departed, Marla left Afghanistan too. She wouldn't be gone for long.

Chapter 5

Portraits of Grief

(How to Get Civilian War Victims on TV)

Hi, everybody! I'm Marla. I represent Global Exchange, and we're bringing some relatives of the 9/11 victims to Afghanistan to meet with Afghan victims in their homes. Would you guys be interested in coming?
—MARLA, ADDRESSING A CROWD OF JOURNALISTS
AT A UN PRESS CONFERENCE, KABUL, JANUARY 2002

Marla returned to San Francisco in mid–December 2001 for the holidays. As always, it wasn't much of a break. She was busy making arrangements again, but this time, she wasn't preparing a rally or media event. She was moving to Kabul in two weeks.

Marla argued that she would be of much better use to Global Exchange's efforts calling attention to civilian casualties by positioning herself in Kabul. Once it was evident that Marla wouldn't take no for an answer, Medea began helping her strategize. They decided the best thing to do was hold private fund-raising events in San Francisco and then funnel the money to individual families who had been harmed or had lost relatives and homes by U.S. bombs. Medea would work with the Afghan community and other sympathetic individuals in California to raise the funds, while Marla would do the legwork on the ground to identify the victims. Medea began working on a plan that she hoped would raise the profile of the Afghan victims. To pull it off, she needed Marla to carry out her best stunt yet. Marla would return to Afghanistan as an independent contractor for Global Exchange.

One night, a small group gathered at a bar near the edge of the San Francisco Bay. Friends noticed a marked change in Marla. Just weeks before, San Francisco had been the center of her universe. By late December, she'd already outgrown it. Marla drank and toasted her friends under the Bay Bridge, the halos of headlights illuminating the fog above, but her thoughts were thousands of miles away.

Nancy picked Marla up from Reno airport near Lake Tahoe, just over the border in Nevada. The family owned a time-share in posh Incline Village, located in the Sierra Nevada mountain range, where they spent most Christmases on the powdery ski slopes. They drove to the Lone Eagle Grille at the lakeshore Hyatt Regency Hotel for dinner, where they met up with the rest of the Ruzickas.

Marla had only a handful of days to spend with her family before she headed back to Afghanistan. They were concerned yet characteristically supportive. Cliff only asked her to please exercise good judgment.

✿ ✿ ✿

The dingy room was packed with bearded men in skullcaps and women dressed in bright *shalwar kameez* ensembles, the billowy blouse and pants outfits worn in Pakistan. They were all contending for a patch of dirty floor space next to the baggage carousel at Islamabad airport. Marla tried to wriggle her way past entire families pointing and shouting in Urdu. As she craned her neck to survey the mountains of suitcases and electronics merchandise creaking by, she spotted someone who didn't fit in and marched toward him.

"Are you a journalist?" Marla asked the Western stranger.

"Yes, I am," he responded in an American accent, slightly taken aback.

"Are you a photographer?" she asked, glimpsing his camera bags.

Right again.

She began chirping away about Afghanistan and her last trip in. She couldn't wait to get back. Thorne Anderson was headed in the same direction. In the weeks following the Taliban's defeat, a UN passenger plane had begun shuttling staff and other paying expatriate customers in between Islamabad and Kabul. Marla and Thorne knew they could be stranded in Islamabad for several days while jostling for the prized six-hundred-dollar seats. She had plans to meet up with her friend Mark Kukis, who had an apartment in Islamabad, and suggested Thorne come along. They jumped into a taxi and sped toward the Marriott Hotel in town to meet Mark Kukis.

Marla had met Mark two weeks earlier in Islamabad when she was on her way back home to California for Christmas. They had spent a wild evening together in the

Marriott's underground bar and dance club, the Bassment. At the time, the American freelance journalist had just tried, and failed, to enter Afghanistan and was sulking with some photojournalists over a few beers. As they sat nursing their wounds, an all-American blonde materialized at their table, seemingly out of nowhere.

Marla had stopped by the Bassment to have some fun—and scope out the journalist scene—before her flight back to San Francisco the next day. The Bassment was one of the only establishments in the Pakistani capital selling booze. Marla entered the dim club and zoomed in on a group of young Western men. She came over and introduced herself.

The men forgot their woes in a cascade of Marla's banter. They talked and drank and laughed, but they were unclear as to what exactly she was doing there on her own. She wasn't a journalist, but she wasn't exactly an aid worker either. At the end of the night, they all exchanged e-mails and hailed a cab home, dropping Marla off in one of the city's nicer neighborhoods. As her door slammed shut and she waved good night, the journalists looked at each other and said, "Who the hell was that?"

For every war or natural disaster, there is a hotel made famous. In Islamabad, the Marriott was the nerve center for the expatriate community. With the war unfolding next door, the city quickly became the main base camp in Pakistan for the media and the United Nations, which held press conferences at the hotel. Mark stopped by the Marriott on most days to read the *International Herald Tribune*. He lit up when Marla, with a Western man by her side, bounced into the Marriott.

Mark was glad for the company. They went to his place,

where Thorne and Marla shared a mattress in a platonic arrangement. She was as fitful asleep as awake, kicking and thrashing throughout the night.

The next week was a blur of long dinners and nights on the town with Thorne, Mark, and a few of his friends. At Marla's urging, the evenings inevitably ended with the group tumbling into the Marriott's Bassment, where she could dance. One night Marla, Thorne, and two others crashed an elaborate Pakistani wedding party at the Marriott after squeezing a few bills into the attending bodyguard's hand. Marla strutted up to the buffet and got in line. She casually chatted with the legitimate guests as if she belonged there too, piling her plate high with delicacies. They polished off their free meals as Pakistani "house" music started thumping. Marla grabbed Thorne and led him onto the empty dance floor. As they twisted and twirled, Marla surveyed the room. Exquisitely dressed Pakistanis sat stiffly in their chairs, watching.

"Look at them," Marla said to Thorne. "They're so beautiful! They look like they want to dance!"

With the words still hanging in the air, she sashayed up to a couple of guests. Grasping their hands, she pulled them onto their feet. Within minutes the dance floor was shimmering with glittering gowns and swaying hips.

New Year's Eve was like any of the other nights in Islamabad—except that Marla's grandiosity reached new heights. It was her twenty-fifth birthday, and she was doing her fair share of celebrating. Mark said that it was the first time he saw her "with the wheels coming off."

Marla weaved her way off the dance floor and over to the

booth Mark was occupying. She plopped down across from him, taking his face firmly in her hands.

"Oh my God, you're *soooo* wonderful, you're *soooo* great!" she slurred.

Growing concerned, Mark and Thorne took Marla back to the apartment, where she staggered into the bedroom and promptly passed out.

The next day, Thorne and Marla, having charmed a UN attendant into assigning them a couple of coveted seats on that flight to Kabul, waited for the shuttle pickup at the UN offices. They were informed that the flight was canceled. It was a common occurrence. Marla took advantage of the disappointing news. In the same way she met Thorne, Marla "picked up" two new friends who were booked on their canceled flight. That night, she and Thorne had dinner with their fellow travelers, a man smuggling DVDs to a women's group in Afghanistan and *Los Angeles Times* staff photographer Rick Loomis.

They had better luck the next day. After landing at Bagram Air Base, the main coalition military center just north of Kabul, Marla hopped down the stairs and onto the concrete tarmac with her twenty or so new friends, gripping a stack of business cards. She had spent the hour-long flight going up and down the aisles, networking. Grabbing her bags, she ducked into a UN vehicle with Thorne and Rick.

"Can you take us to the Mustafa Hotel?" they asked.

Kabul's new journalist hub boasted a small restaurant, which felt more like a living room than a public gathering space. Guests used buckets of heated water to bathe. The "walls" separating the rooms were nothing more than freshly installed glass window panes that had been painted. They didn't have reservations, and there were only two vacant rooms left. Marla paired up with Rick, while Thorne shared a room with someone else. Marla and Rick planned to bunk together at the Mustafa for one night, which turned into a couple of weeks after he realized how broke she was.

Marla had cashed in her savings account and stuffed the wad, about three thousand dollars, into her pocket when she left San Francisco. Medea had agreed to send Marla money in small increments, which she could draw on for giving donations to civilian war victims and to pay her own expenses. But she wasn't earning a salary, and the costly visas and plane tickets had already whittled away a good chunk of her reserves. As rudimentary as the accommodations were in Kabul, hotel and property owners were enjoying the fruits of supply and demand. Western journalists and aid agencies with inflated expense accounts spilled into town every day, and the cost of living began to skyrocket. Marla crashed on a number of floors and mattresses in January, using her limited funds to get down to business.

On one of her first days back in Kabul, Marla walked down Chicken Street looking for a jewelery shop. Despite its name, the road is no longer known for its poultry. It is now flanked by rows of shops displaying traditional jewelry, decorative daggers and lanterns, colorful fringed rugs, and general bric-a-brac. Kabul's new foreign residents arrived there looking for exotic Afghan souvenirs or gifts for friends and family back home. After passing rows of small kiosks, Marla found and entered the small store, where Ahmad Hashimi was waiting for her.

Ahmad was working as a translator and journalist assistant, known as a "fixer," when the twenty-year-old Afghan met Marla at a *Newsweek* party in Kabul. A rare commodity in Kabul, Ahmad's English skills landed him gigs with several big media outfits, including the *New York Times*, *Newsweek*, and the British Broadcasting Corporation (BBC). He was sharp and friendly, and his English was basic but passable. She asked him if he'd work with her, and he agreed. She needed help, fast.

On January 16, Medea would arrive in Kabul alongside four family members of Americans who died in the September 11 terrorist attacks. The grieving relatives were sympathetic to Afghans who had similarly lost loved ones during the U.S. bombing campaign. It was a controversial visit that Medea knew would attract media attention.

It was Marla's job to organize everything for the high-profile delegation, and it would be a formidable feat to pull off in Kabul, where it often proved impossible to accomplish even the most basic tasks. With Ahmad's knowledge and assistance, she visited hospitals, orphanages, and women's projects to scout out site visits for the delegation's weeklong trip. Marla also had to find decent lodging for everyone in a city with no vacant hotel rooms. She needed to track down Afghan war victims in a country with few telephones. Above all, Marla was expected to make the delegation's visit an international media event. At least she knew where to find the journalists.

Rory Carroll, the Irish correspondent for the British *Guardian* newspaper had arranged for his driver to take him, *Houston Chronicle* reporter John Otis, and an Afghan translator to the village of Qalaye Niazi in Paktia Province, which had been bombed the week before. He was less than thrilled about squeezing another body into their small car, but John had told Marla about their planned trip the night before and she invited herself along. When Marla eagerly stumbled into the Mustafa's lobby before sunrise, Rory reluctantly agreed to take her with them.

They climbed into the car and drove southeast through the darkened streets, skittish but excited. They rarely escaped Kabul. All the action was taking place on Afghanistan's eastern flank, where U.S. bombers continued their campaign to annihilate al-Qaeda and remnants of the Taliban. Marla was sandwiched between the American correspondent and Rory.

After a few hours, they reached Qalaye Niazi, a small hamlet outside of Gardez, the explosive province's capital.

They paid a visit to residents living in a section of the village that had escaped the strike. Marla listened attentively but was quiet, allowing her more experienced companions to do the talking. Another section of the village was completely wiped out. Their neighbors weren't sure of the exact number of casualties; the bodies had already been laid to rest. Marla, Rory, John, and their Afghan translator walked through the remains, finding a woman's scalp with gray braided hair. Small chunks of charred flesh mingled with pieces of candy and wedding decorations. They carefully weaved around unexploded bombs littering the area.

The afternoon was growing late. They wanted to return before nightfall and started back toward Kabul. Marla chatted effusively on the ride home, praising the journalists for their reporting skills and winning new allies.

In the evenings Marla's fun side went into overdrive. She caught up with Rick Loomis, Thorne Anderson, and the other journalists at the Mustafa and, within a week or so, blossomed into the hotel's entertainment director.

Marla brightened the hotel, helping to transform the dreary collection of rooms into a home of sorts. She encouraged parties—often including salsa dancing in the small restaurant. The Afghan staff looked on, dumbfounded. Journalists paid a fortune for alcohol on nearby Chicken Street, and soon the Mustafa got wise and began selling beer at twelve dollars per can. As the party got going, Marla would hop from one stressed-out journalist to the next, gripping his or her neck and shoulders. Her fingers kneaded their tense muscles. All the while she chatted and giggled with the journalists like they were old friends.

Although she was well-connected at the Mustafa, Marla wanted to extend her reach to Kabul's broader community of media. A good place to start was at another, bigger hotel.

The Intercontinental Hotel's architects had a dream of turning it into a world-class establishment. Years of war had left it rotting instead. The hotel received few visitors—until now. The UN press conferences at the Intercontinental were crammed with hungry journalists on the prowl for stories.

At one such conference, Stephanie Bunker shouted statistics on refugees and starving families to the journalists. The UN spokeswoman's hands clenched the lectern as she tried to yell louder, a wool pakol hat perched on her head. There was very little electricity and no heat, every major news organization elbowed for a spot at the UN press conferences in those early days.

Stephanie finished and the crowd splintered. She was circulating among the usual hardened suspects when Marla jumped in front of her.

"Hi! That was a great presentation! I'm Marla, and I'm also here doing human rights work, trying to help people hurt by the bombs," she said breathlessly.

Stephanie stared in astonishment at the young woman in front of her. Marla continued to rattle off information about Global Exchange.

Approaching Stephanie was a savvy move. Like Pam Constable of the *Washington Post*, Stephanie was an American who had worked in the region for years. She was one of the media's top sources on humanitarian operations and the toll the war was taking on civilians in Afghanistan. Every journalist courted her for information, and between cigarettes, she banged out one interview after another. Marla handed her some Global Exchange pamphlets and then bounced away. Stephanie normally would have thrown them in the trash, but something about Marla compelled her to hold on to them. Days later Marla had her own turn at the lectern.

* * *

Omar Samad, the new spokesman at the Afghan Foreign Ministry, introduced Marla to the crowd. She skipped up to the Intercontinental's lectern, faced a crowd of Western faces, and smiled.

"Hi everybody! I'm Marla! I represent Global Exchange, and we're bringing some relatives of the 9/11 victims to Afghanistan to meet with Afghan victims in their homes. Would you guys be interested in coming?"

The audience perked up and collectively shouted, "Yes!"

NBC News producer Rachel Levin surveyed the pack at the press conference. She turned to her correspondent. They both had the same thought: *Every network in town is going to want dibs on this story, and there will be more cameras than victims.*

"Have you ever heard of something called a pool?" Rachel asked Marla, pulling her aside.

"Um, no, I don't think so. What is it?"

"Well, you're going to have more media than interaction with the Afghan people if you let everyone cover it. You need one camera in the Afghan family's house, and then we'll all share."

Grateful for the useful tip, she showered Rachel with thanks and then left to make arrangements with the other journalists who wanted to cover the story.

Marla met Medea and the four September 11 family members as they descended the plane at Bagram Air Base on January 16. The media lurked in the background. Medea scanned the tarmac for Colin Powell; she had heard that the

U.S. secretary of state was due in Kabul soon and assumed the journalists were waiting for his arrival. The delegation was discussing this when Marla turned to them, beaming with pride.

"No, no! They're here for *you*, not Colin Powell!"

Medea wanted a strong turnout during their site visits, but this was over the top. Stunned, the group of grieving family members stared at the journalists.

And then they were off to meet their first Afghan victim, the media in tow. With her assistant Ahmad's help, Marla had arranged for the September 11 relatives to visit Najiba Shakar Pardes, who had been buried under rubble in her home after a bomb struck her residential neighborhood on October 17.

The September 11 family members squeezed past the television crews and into the bare room.

Rita Lasar, a seventy-year-old New Yorker, lost her brother, Abe Zelmanowitz, at One World Trade Center. He was on the twenty-seventh floor and could have saved himself, but instead stayed behind with a colleague confined to a wheelchair. President Bush invoked Abe's heroic act in a speech honoring the dead at the National Cathedral.

Derrill Bodley's only child, twenty-year-old Deora, was killed when United Airlines Flight 93 plunged into a Pennsylvania field. Deora was flying home to California on September 11 to visit her father. The fifty-six-year-old musician composed a song on September 13 to express his grief. He played "Steps to Peace—For Deora" on his keyboard at a White House tribute and gave a copy of the CD to the president. Derrill's stepdaughter Eva Rupp, a federal government employee in Washington, D.C., joined him on the trip to Afghanistan.

Kelly Campbell's twenty-eight-year-old brother-in-law, Craig Amundson, was killed at the Pentagon. The soldier's widow, Amber, had been outspoken about reconciliation, not retribution, in the wake of the terrorist attacks. The family didn't feel that bombing Afghanistan, where civilians would die, was the right response to Craig's death. Campbell, who was twenty-nine at the time, is on the steering committee of Peaceful Tomorrows, an organization founded by family members of those killed on September 11 that advocates a nonviolent pursuit of justice. She traveled with Global Exchange to Afghanistan on behalf of Craig's widow, who was at home caring for her two small children.

Rita, Derrill, Eva, and Kelly sat down on a red Afghan carpet, one of Najiba's only remaining belongings. They listened to the traumatized thirty-eight-year-old quietly recount the day when the U.S. bomb left her body broken and her face disfigured. Miraculously, her husband and three children escaped unharmed. They were homeless, living in cramped quarters with friends.

Najiba had spent weeks in the hospital and the family had received no compensation for her injuries or the accidental destruction of their home, which the impoverished family had no means of rebuilding. No one had apologized— until now. The September 11 delegates expressed their sympathies for their suffering, and the family reciprocated the sentiment. The journalists were handed a poignant human interest story, telling a broader tale of the war's suffering, which their editors were sure to run.

On their second day, Marla had again arranged a rigorous schedule visiting civilian war victims in town. The Intercontinental was the starting line, and a group of journalists took their positions out front. The September 11 delegation pulled onto the road and they were off. The journalists urged their drivers to speed up, kicking up thick clouds of dust. With only inches between them, they swerved past one another on the rutted roads. Everyone wanted to arrive at the house first to get front-row seats.

Mohammed Rahaf talked to Rita, Derrill, Eva, and Kelly in front of the glaring lights and TV lenses. Along with his thirteen-year-old brother, Azizullah, and nine-year-old sister, Sabera, the twenty-six-year-old had been relying on friends and neighbors for food and shelter since U.S. bombs destroyed their home in another residential district of Kabul. They hadn't been as lucky as Najiba's family. Their mother, grandmother, a brother, a sister, and her husband had been killed in the accidental strike. The delegates gave Azizullah a soccer ball, Sabera a dress, and Mohammed words of encouragement. They would lobby the U.S. government for help.

Amin Said's newly wedded brother and sister-in-law were killed when an errant bomb smashed into the side of his house. Rita and Amin, who both lost siblings, shared their stories of grief. Amin requested a moment of silence in remembrance of Abe Zelmanowitz of Brooklyn and Iqbal and Zarlash Said of Kabul. Amin bowed his head while Rita covered her face with her hands and cried. The thirty-six-year-old man gently led her into a bright room spread with cushions and rugs.

"He was your brother, but he was also my brother. We are all brothers and sisters," Amin told Rita.

They continued talking for a few moments longer before it was time to leave.

Outside, Marla was surrounded by a crowd of Afghans who were talking about their suffering. She rushed from families to reporters, eventually gravitating to a crowd of children who were mesmerized by her blond hair and playfulness. She was a child herself in their company.

Marla's resourcefulness impressed the delegation. She had found a few beds for the group in an NGO's guesthouse close to the recently reopened U.S. embassy. She booked Rita, the eldest in the group, into the Intercontinental, which the delegation wrongly assumed was the most luxurious option in town. She hired two drivers, who chauffeured them around Kabul in a Toyota and a beat-up minivan.

There were a couple of vegetarians on the trip, so Marla promised a special feast for the group. She bought fresh produce in a local market and asked the Mustafa's kitchen staff to prepare a vegetarian meal. Scratching their heads, the cooks boiled the vegetables into a viscous stew. Marla was so pleased when the dish was served that the delegates couldn't bring themselves to disappoint her. Stirring the mash on his plate, Derrill finally broke the silence.

"Marla, I'm sorry, but I can't eat this. It's inedible," he said apologetically, putting down his fork.

"Oh, no, I'm sorry! You're right, though. It totally sucks!" Marla laughed before growing quiet, lost in thought.

"I know! We can eat soup tomorrow instead!" she announced after a few seconds.

Other preparations were equally improvised. With little communication in the country, Marla arranged meetings by sending scribbled notes to homes and offices with a driver. The delegates often grew nervous that their plans would fall flat, but time and again Marla pulled through at the last second.

The American embassy in Kabul had reopened shortly before the delegates arrived. Like many Third World nations, Afghanistan had been a Cold War battlefield. The Soviet Union invaded the country in 1979 and gave birth to the mujahideen, a breed of Islamic guerrilla fiercely opposed to occupation. Strengthened by American assistance, the mujahideen bludgeoned the Soviet troops over the next decade. The Soviets finally retreated in 1989, and a brutal civil war continued between the Soviet-backed communist government and the U.S.-supported mujahideen. Anarchy closed in on Kabul with a near-total breakdown of law and order. The American diplomatic corps left town in a hurry, shutting the embassy doors in early 1989. The Americans found petrified food in the refrigerator and half-smoked cigars still resting in an ashtray when they moved back in. Black cobwebs clung to the walls and ceiling. As the delegation toured the building, they talked with the acting ambassador about the tragic Afghan stories. The relatives of September 11 victims' voices carried weight, and the ambassador suggested they carefully document specific cases where civilians had been harmed or killed. If they brought the information back, the embassy would see what it could do.

Derrill and Eva returned home to their jobs, but Rita, Kelly, and Medea stayed on with Marla for several more days. They devised a rough survey form and revisited families they had already met. They gathered precise information about the incidents, filling in the blanks with details: date and place of bombing, names and ages of people harmed or killed, the nature of injuries or death, type of property damage, and so on.

Thus was born the first Afghan civilian casualty survey, in the tattered notebooks of Americans still grieving the loss of their own loved ones.

The group met one woman whose story turned their sorrow into anger. The delegation was visiting one of the UN World Food Program's female-run bakeries, which provided affordable bread and jobs for widows, when they met Arifa. She had lost eight relatives in a U.S. attack just two blocks away from the bakery. She recounted the story, moving the Americans to tears.

In her desperation, Arifa wrote a letter to the American government explaining what had happened to her family. She didn't know who else to turn to, so she brought it to the U.S. embassy. She never made it past the gate. Assuming Arifa was a beggar, the embassy guards turned her away.

Even if the guards had accepted the letter, there was

nobody in particular to deliver it to. There was no civilian casualty office at the embassy, and no policy existed for compensating civilian war victims.

Rita Lasar was so distraught by Arifa's story that the group decided to bring her to the embassy themselves. Medea invited the press. But the U.S. government was not as enthusiastic about discussing delicate matters in public. The delegates turned in their survey forms at the gate and proffered Arifa's letter. The U.S. Marine guard took that, too. However, the delegates were not allowed back into the embassy. It seemed they were no longer welcome.

The delegation's confrontational tactics may have created a media stir, but they also shut the door on discussing civilian casualty compensation, even if it had only been open a crack. The delegates never met with the acting ambassador again. With or without the government's help, the group decided to establish their own Afghan victims' fund. They decided the best way to do this was to conduct a nationwide survey that would identify the victims. The tally would include personal stories as well as statistics, culminating in an Afghan "Portraits of Grief" report, named after the poignant series of September 11 obituaries printed daily in the *New York Times*. Marla volunteered to take on this unprecedented project, organizing teams of surveyors in Afghanistan. Global Exchange and Peaceful Tomorrows, the organization cofounded by Kelly Campbell and other September 11 family members, would both fund the project.

Shortly before the delegation's departure, Marla and Ahmad arranged a meeting at their guesthouse with Afghan

NGOs and officials to seek advice about financial compensation for civilian war victims. Through the usual system of notes, everyone arrived at the appropriate hour and gathered in a small conference room. Afghan culture dictates that a host must offer guests tea and preferably some sort of sweets. Hospitality is simply a given for Afghanistan's dignified people, no matter how poor. Marla had ordered tea and cookies for the meeting, but they hadn't arrived. The Afghans fidgeted and looked uncomfortable, and so did their American hostesses. Where was the tea? They couldn't start the meeting without it. Marla went to check with the guesthouse staff. The treats had been placed in the wrong room. Everyone sighed with relief, the tea was poured, the cookies distributed, and the discussion began.

The meeting eventually led to a team of surveyors. Marla was referred to reliable candidates and hired fifteen Afghans, many of them professional engineers. Under her supervision, Ahmad would be the team leader arranging the difficult details of the surveyors' daily duties. Meanwhile, Marla would do what she did best.

Chapter 6

Club Kabul

(How to Survive on a
Shoestring in a War Zone)

The United States spent thirty million dollars a day bombing Afghanistan, now we think it is the responsibility of Americans to help the civilian victims.
—MARLA SPEAKING AT A NEWS CONFERENCE IN FRONT OF
THE U.S. EMBASSY, KABUL, FEBRUARY 2002

By late January 2002, Marla was fast becoming the unrivaled queen bee of Kabul's social life. Parties at the Mustafa became more frequent as more journalists and other Westerners arrived in town. Characters like Jack Idema, an American civilian in dark sunglasses and military fatigues, joined the mix. When he wasn't attending parties in Kabul, he hunted for Osama bin Laden and his men in Afghanistan's hidden corners and crevices. The journalists' workloads had also lightened a bit. The news had quieted down after the Afghan interim government, chaired by Hamid Karzai, took over in December. By nine p.m. most journalists had finished filing their daily stories and rushed over to the Mustafa to enjoy a can of twelve-dollar beer, good music, and company before the ten-thirty citywide curfew began. For Marla, they were great networking opportunities as well as an excuse to have a little fun with people she genuinely adored. She needed them to get her work done.

Alfons Luna, a Spanish reporter working for the French news agency Agence France-Presse (AFP) was the last of the AFP bureau to meet Marla, but they became fast friends. Although he thought she was an attractive girl, he quickly developed protective, fatherly feelings for her. The two met through his AFP colleagues Bryan Pearson, a South African writer who covered the September 11 visit, and Jimin Lai, a young photographer from Malaysia. Alfons was glad to discover Marla; until then, the AFP bureau's social life consisted of watching BBC World and MTV.

There was a shortage of women in Kabul's expatriate community. Normally aloof males metamorphosed into aggressive suitors at Marla's parties. She nudged anyone who dared to be shy or self-doubting.

Marla had a crush on Jimin, and the feelings were mutual. Alfons had his eye on Nina Biddle, a statuesque blonde who wrote for *People*. She was new in town and staying at the Mustafa, where the Spaniard had glimpsed her.

On the evening of January 25, Jimin and Alfons had a date with a bottle of Uzbek vodka, Nina, and Marla. The last of the delegation had just left, and Marla was able to focus on new projects. Marla and Jimin's eyes had met across a crowded press conference or two, and they had spoken a few times. That night, she was planning on taking the charged glances and small talk to another level.

But Jimin, whose frenetic energy challenged Marla's, soon became distracted from the evening's goal. He and fellow photographer Paula Bronstein engaged in a lengthy work conversation in her room, along with some other journalists. Marla periodically skipped over to check on him, her hand around the bottle of vodka. The party moved into Paula's room.

The journalists sipped beer and smoked cigarettes as they talked. A small space heater buzzed in the corner. Wrapped in her heavy coat, Nina sat down next to Alfons on the sofa. They discovered they had a lot in common. He was from Barcelona, where she had lived as a child, and they began chatting in Spanish. Just before curfew, Alfons got up to leave.

After he left, Nina briefed Marla on the coincidence that she and Alfons were from the same city.

"Why don't you two have a *romance*!" Marla declared in the roomful of journalists.

"Oh, don't be ridiculous!" Nina responded, blushing.

Alfons and Nina would be married less than a year later.

Marla left town the next day to start investigating uncharted territory while Ahmad kept busy setting up a surveyor team, which would be collecting civilian casualty data across the country. As usual, Marla had to be creative. Journalists and aid agencies were spending tens of thousands of dollars to ensure their staff was adequately equipped—and protected—to operate successfully in Afghanistan. Only the most intrepid of freelancers braved Afghanistan's harsh, militia-infested terrain without a satellite phone, translator, and flak jacket. And those were normally tough men. Marla hitched a ride to the northern city of Mazar-i-Sharif with BBC radio journalist Quil Lawrence who had been her salsa dancing partner at the Mustafa. He was wary because she still came off as reckless, but he gave in to her cheerful pleas.

Road trips in Afghanistan were always risky, but more so in the wintertime. Reaching Mazar meant passing through the treacherous Salang Tunnel. Avalanches falling from the mountains above often sealed the damaged tunnel shut, creating a death trap. The fumes alone in the traffic-clogged passageway could cause asphyxiation. Quil decided that if they didn't clear the tunnel, which is more than a mile in length, by two p.m., they'd turn back for Kabul. One hour after leaving Kabul, they got stuck in a snow bank before even reaching the tunnel. Quil told Marla they might be forced to spend the night in their sleeping bags.

"Oh, I don't have a sleeping bag!" she said.

Quil looked at her in disbelief; she must have been the only foreigner in the country without a survival kit. Luckily they freed themselves just in time to reach their goal. Emerging from the tunnel, Quil decided to forge ahead to Mazar. Marla talked about how she fooled her parents into thinking she was going to London on her first trip to Afghanistan, and Quil recorded her. They were soon delayed again by a stalled truck on the road. Dusk fell. It was definitely not a good thing to be stranded in the middle of an Afghan mountain range on an arctic night.

They had two options: freeze to death in their car or find shelter somewhere in the closest village. As they drove by roadhouses full of Afghan men, Quil instructed her to hide in his sleeping bag on the floor. Marla didn't have a head scarf, and her blond hair was a liability that could get her raped or worse, but she remained cool. Following Afghan protocol, Quil thought it was best to check in with the local governor to avoid getting killed. It was a good call. They ended up spending the night at the warlord's compound. The guards lent them their room, which had a small woodstove. It was better than the car. Before they went to sleep, Marla gave Quil a back rub. His translator looked on, shocked.

Once in Mazar the next morning, Marla and Quil parted ways. Quil was there to interview General Abdul Rashid Dostum, the region's notorious Uzbek warlord, and hunt down some other stories. Marla just wanted to poke around and network. She waved good-bye and wandered off alone. The sight of the solitary Western woman weaving through the streets of Mazar left the locals frozen in their footsteps. The traditional people of Mazar—many women were still shrouded in burkas and men in turbans—had never seen anything like it. It was unheard of and few, if any, other Western women would have felt at such ease. Marla hopped along, happy to be out among the Afghan people even if she couldn't speak the language. Her friendly smile was communication enough. Focused on work, she was indifferent to what people thought and didn't burden herself with security concerns. Later that day, Quil spotted her from the protection of his car: a poorly covered blond head bobbing down the street on the edge of town, on her own without a translator.

Another Western radio correspondent who knew Marla from Kabul had also made the perilous trek to Mazar. He and an Afghan colleague took a moment to do some sightseeing at the city's sacred Shrine of Hazrat Ali. As he diverted his gaze from the indigo blue and turquoise mosaic, a blond mirage entered his vision. Marla walked across the courtyard, a huge grin on her face. They talked for a minute, and the much older man was overcome by a sudden urge to protect her. But she had things to do and vanished as suddenly as she had appeared.

Destitute but intent on carrying out her mission in Afghanistan, Marla began relying more systematically on the foreign correspondents. When she returned from Mazar, she moved into the Agence France-Presse compound in Kabul's affluent Wazir Akbar Khan district. High-paying news agencies snatched up the neighborhood's spacious Western-style houses, turning their rent-collecting owners into very rich men by Afghan standards. Marla laid claim to the AFP basement, where she slept on a borrowed mattress after long days documenting civilian casualties with Ahmad. By the time she returned from Mazar, Jimin had left for Malaysia, but Alfons was still in town.

Normally territorial, journalists happily shared their space, food, and office equipment with Marla. It was an unspoken, symbiotic relationship; she brightened their day, and they paid the rent. Their charity provided a crutch for

Marla's budget, while her guilelessness melted their competitive hearts.

The AFP reporters stumbled bleary-eyed to their computers each morning, where a personal note written in Marla's flowery script was waiting on their keyboards. Marla would already be gone for the day, visiting families and making contacts. Unfolding their scraps of paper, the reporters smiled at her words, the i's dotted with hearts. No doubt she'd already fired off a few e-mails to San Francisco from one of their computers.

Marla joined Bryan Pearson, the South African AFP reporter she had befriended, on jogging expeditions through Kabul's potholed streets. Her uncovered blond hair turned disbelieving Afghan heads wherever they went. In the evenings, the bureau gathered around the dinner table. Marla barely touched her food. Initially, the Afghan house staff disapproved of the boisterous American guest who wasn't contributing to their salaries. Despite the language barrier and their grumbling, Marla made an effort to be kind with the cooks and drivers. Her friendliness soon chipped away at their resentment, turning frowns into laughter.

An AFP reporter told Marla about Sahib Dad. Like Arifa, the woman the September 11 delegation brought to the embassy, he was also living near the communication tower that the U.S. bombers had targeted in early October. Shortly before dawn, Sahib lay asleep in bed alongside his wife in the three-room house they shared with their four children. The screech of approaching airplanes jolted him awake. He ran outside and down the street to see where the bombs were falling. The sky was still dark. Sahib didn't know a bomb had crumbled his own home until a neighbor pointed to black smoke unfurling from his property. He rushed back to find two rooms totally destroyed and one damaged. His wife, Rahila, was crying, blood spouting from her head. The neighbors took her to the hospital while he scavenged through the rubble for his children. When he found them, two were injured but alive, their son Hussain, seven, and their three-year-old daughter Sajjia. Their four-year-old son, Ali Sajjad, and two-year-old daughter, Freshta, had been crushed to death by a collapsed wall.

The AFP reporter, who was also Afghan, had interviewed Sahib for a news story. The reporter was so saddened by Sahib's loss that he offered him a job washing dishes and preparing breakfast in a guesthouse he had opened for foreigners. Sahib accepted and moved the family away from their neighborhood. Marla interviewed Sahib and Rahila in their new one-room dwelling. Marla cried throughout the interview and gave them a hundred dollars on her way out, with promises to help more soon.

Marla began paying Arifa regular visits, and they became friends. Shortly after the September 11 delegation met her in her home, Marla returned with a journalist. They drove up the steep hill, which was littered with earthen-colored hovels.

After they arrived, Marla yelled from the street, "Arifa! Arifa! Arifa!"

The woman emerged, happy and amazed to see the

American girl again. Marla rushed toward Arifa, hugging her for several minutes.

Arifa led Marla and the journalist into her small home. While the journalist scribbled Arifa's story in his notebook, Marla played and laughed with her children and gave them an armful of toys she had scrounged up in town. She never showed up empty-handed.

In one short month, Marla, Ahmad, and the team of surveyors had located dozens of Afghans like Arifa in and around Kabul who had lost family members or been injured by the U.S. bombs. They had worked tirelessly, digging through heaps of hospital records and talking to everyone in town to find them. Marla and Ahmad, with the help of an Afghan aid agency, gathered the victims to discuss their right to compensation. On February 13, Marla led a group of these victims, including Arifa and Sahib, in a demonstration outside the U.S. Embassy.

"The Afghan government does not have the funds to do it and the U.S. government has shown no inclination to do it!" Marla yelled as she punched her fist in the air. The group of grieving and harmed Afghans glared beside her.

Marla demanded that the United States create a twenty-million-dollar fund to compensate civilian war victims.

"The United States spent thirty million dollars a day bombing Afghanistan, now we think it is the responsibility of Americans to help the civilian victims!" Marla cried, her blond hair exposed.

"Come out and talk to us! You bombed these families, and it's your responsibility to help them!" she shouted.

She had recruited much of Kabul's international press corps to attend the show. The journalists, Alfons among them, hovered around her snapping photographs and taking notes. He later said that was the moment when Marla's real fame began. She had some help from her friends, who spread the story around the world.

Alfons reported that the U.S. government had earmarked one million dollars to pay medical expenses for Afghans who had lost limbs in the bombing. The funds had yet to materialize, and doctors' bills were just a drop of the assistance Afghan victims needed. The Pentagon claimed it was "putting together a paper" on civilian casualties but wouldn't address the issue of compensation. Because collecting information was so difficult, estimates of civilian deaths from October through December ranged from one thousand to nearly four thousand. Marla officially announced to the crowd that she would manage a nationwide survey of civilian casualties.

The surveys would not only produce a number but also identify the names and faces of civilians who needed help. Her team would soon begin the difficult tallies beyond Kabul, in eastern provinces like Paktia, Khost, and Nangarhar, where many bombing raids occurred.

In front of the razor wire that looped around the embassy, the aggrieved Afghans recounted their stories. Arifa tearfully addressed reporters. A father spoke of his daughter who was killed when a bomb landed in a street where she was playing. Azizullah's leg was sliced off by shrapnel. In an instant, the twenty-one-year-old handyman who supported eight relatives had become unemployable.

"The victims need homes now. Azizullah needs a leg now. They can't wait months and months," Marla told the gathering.

Arifa and Sahib said that despite Marla's pleas, nobody talked to them. They returned with Marla on several occasions, and the embassy shooed them away—and told them to stay away. If any financial assistance arrived, they would be notified. The Afghans were disheartened, and so was Marla.

Marla's end goal was finding practical assistance for hurt families. Yet she wasn't friends with those who had the means, and the dollars, to help. The embassy probably viewed Marla's confrontational line of attack as a nuisance in postconflict Kabul, and her calls for a compensation fund continued to go unanswered. Despite her good intentions, she never got through the gate.

She did succeed, however, in embarrassing the embassy, and she began drawing international attention to the largely ignored plight of Afghan civilian war victims by inviting legions of journalists to cover the demonstration. Marla hoped the bad publicity would pressure the Americans into taking her request for a fund more seriously. Instead, mocking soldiers dubbed her "Kabul Jane" after Jane Fonda's Vietnam War moniker "Hanoi Jane." Many wrote Marla off as nothing more than an irrational and unpatriotic antiwar protester. Perhaps the embassy assumed she would eventually go away. They didn't know how determined she was.

Marla's surveyors fanned out across Afghanistan's war-scarred terrain and slowly began excavating more stories of human tragedy. It was not easy work for Ahmad, who coordinated the survey teams. Obtaining access to hospital and municipality records, if they existed, was an arduous and sometimes painfully slow process. Homeless families in a country with few street names or addresses had to be found. Permissions needed to be granted by local "authorities" in some of Afghanistan's most volatile regions. When she could, Marla traveled into the dangerous Afghan backwoods with Ahmad, monitoring the work in progress. Multimillion-dollar aid agencies were having a hard enough time operating in Afghanistan, hiring helicopters for tens of thousands of dollars to reach remote areas, assessing the food and medical needs of war-affected people. Marla and Ahmad, who was barely an adult, had a beat-up taxi and a small handful of cash.

Medea grew increasingly frustrated with Marla as 2002 progressed. Both Global Exchange and Peaceful Tomorrows were funding the surveys, and Medea agreed to allocate $20,000 toward the project, based on a budget outline provided by Marla. Back in San Francisco, she held private fundraisers for the surveys and Afghan victims. She agreed to send Marla the cash as she needed it. In return, Marla was told to provide Global Exchange with written reports detailing the civilian casualty information she and her teams were gathering. Her coffers ran dry quickly. Stacks of Afghani bills easily slipped through her fingers when she visited civilian victims, who, she thought, needed the money more than she did.

Marla repeatedly assured Medea that the reports were forthcoming, or already in the mail. They never arrived. Donors wanted to see the fruit of their contributions, but Medea had nothing to show them. Her money transfers to

Afghanistan became more sporadic. Their relationship, already weakened by Marla's decision to stay in Afghanistan and not to go to the Washington, D.C., press conference back in December, began to fester. It never healed.

Marla needed to fatten her bank account quickly. In a flash of entrepreneurial brilliance, Club Kabul was born. It was perhaps the most famous, shortest-lived bar in history.

Technically, Club Kabul was not Afghanistan's first post-Taliban bar. It was, however, Afghanistan's only establishment serving alcohol to paying foreigners (out of respect for Muslim culture, Afghans were not allowed entry), no matter what their profession. The United Nations bar was accessible only to UN employees, with the exception of one night per week when its doors opened to other aid workers. Journalists were not allowed, at least in theory. Floods of foreign aid workers poured into Kabul in February and March, and the crowds swelled at the weekly minglers. Plucky reporters lied their way in or latched onto aid workers. But their attempts at subterfuge didn't guarantee entry. An environment that was more welcoming to her friends would make for a booming business in Kabul, Marla thought. She was right.

An Afghan UN guesthouse manager in the Wazir Akbar Khan neighborhood agreed to provide space for the club in the building's ground floor. Marla spent days preparing the grand opening, scavenging Kabul for alcohol. She had plenty of suppliers. Soldiers with the multinational peacekeeping forces known by the acronym ISAF (International Security Assistance Force) often cut her a deal in return for her friendly flirting. She was also a regular at Chicken Street's Chelsi Market, popular with Kabul's new Western residents. Its owner stocked his shelves high with European and American delicacies, and now sold beer and vodka on the sly. Illicit alcohol was flowing onto Afghanistan's black market from Uzbekistan, and other neighboring countries. Marla had such a good rapport with the owner that he once lent her several hundred dollars when she was in a pinch.

With the inventory in place, Marla strung up Christmas lights, hired a group of Afghan musicians, decided on a cover charge, and recruited a couple of male *Newsweek* reporters to tend bar. Club Kabul's grand opening might have been the toughest day's work the bartending journalists clocked during their tour of Afghanistan. Mobs of their thirsty colleagues shoved into the bar, waving fists full of dollars. Tossing their inhibitions away with their cash, reporters danced to traditional Afghan music while Marla flitted from patron to patron. Western beats blasted from a CD player when the band was on break. It was so packed that revelers overflowed into the street, providing them a back view of the nearby American Embassy. Armed Marines looked on from their fortified perches. A smattering of aid workers and peacekeepers, and even the Italian ambassador, joined in, gleefully throwing down three dollars for the Kabul Sling, a mix of vodka and soda served up in a small plastic cup.

Although Club Kabul was a smashing success, it died a quick death. One of the *Newsweek* bartenders who described the evening in an article wrote that the building owners raised their rent and demanded half the profits after they saw the crowds. An Afghan dressed in police or military uniform showed up the next morning asking for a "permit." What he really wanted was a bribe. There is such a thing as too much good publicity, and Marla had to find a new home for Club Kabul. The night after the grand opening, Marla and a handful of *Newsweek* and AFP reporters gathered in the bar and polished off its last Kabul Sling. She never found another permanent venue, or maybe she simply gave up looking.

Sooner or later Marla always moved on, not wanting to overstay her welcome anywhere. Over the course of the next months, she compound-hopped in Wazir, staying with the NGO Handicap International, ABC News, *Newsweek*, and National Public Radio. She crashed in a number of other houses here and there, and even found refuge for a couple of days with Omar Samad, the Afghan Foreign Ministry spokesman at the time.

Marla walked into Omar's office one day to find out what the Afghans were doing to help the bombing victims. The young American-educated official explained that unfortunately they weren't doing much; the fledgling government was cash-strapped and had an entire country to rebuild after decades of war. But he admired what she was trying to do. She returned on several occasions seeking advice, and they developed a friendship. She trusted the dapper diplomat, and he admired her courage and sincerity. Their talks about civilian casualties broadened into deeper discussions about the war on terror. His perspective of the U.S. bombing clashed with that of the activist community.

Omar occasionally bumped into Marla at parties, and he asked her to his own social gatherings. At one point, the spokesman was temporarily homeless himself and living with friends in Wazir. Marla was transitioning between journalist compounds, and he invited her to crash with him and his friends for a couple of nights. He educated Marla on the complexities of Afghanistan's brutal past and she began to understand that not only was war complicated, but that the U.S. had strived to avoid harming civilians despite many fatal mistakes.

Despite her friction with Medea, Marla continued to act as the public face of Global Exchange in Afghanistan. The organization had timed a high-profile women's delegation to coincide with International Women's Day on March 8, the first Afghanistan would celebrate in twenty-three years. Along with thirteen other professional women, Bianca Jagger, Mick Jagger's former wife, would be in Marla's care for a week. The celebrity activist and native Nicaraguan had been outspoken on human rights issues during the Central American conflicts of the 1980s.

Marla was scrambling to find qualified speakers to talk to the women about bombing victims when she collided with Sam Zia-Zarifi, a legal research director for the New York-based Human Rights Watch, at a party. He already knew her by reputation, and they began chatting. His internationally respected human rights advocacy group had collected some of their own data on civilian casualties after visiting bombing sites with coordinates provided by the Pentagon. Sam told her that although there was a significant number of casualties, it could have been a lot worse. Marla's eyes widened as he spoke. The wheels started spinning in her head. She needed this guy's help.

"Wow, your work's so amazing!" she bubbled, before going in for the kill.

In the same way that she'd lassoed Tony Newman into speaking about Cuba in Lakeport, she lobbied the attorney to speak to the Global Exchange delegation. Too weary to continue fending off her appeals, he gave in.

Keeping his promise, Sam showed up at the guesthouse opposite the U.S. Embassy where the women were staying. He presented the facts, explaining what Human Rights Watch was doing in Afghanistan. They were researching the human cost of the bombing campaign, and what they were finding, he told them, was that the U.S. military's performance was not exactly terrible. Their researchers had checked several bombing sites, and it was becoming clear that the military made efforts to avoid striking civilians.

"Unfortunately, civilians will inevitably die in war, but you have to do the best you can. Had the U.S. been really evil? Well, we're just not finding that," he said.

With help from Ahmad and a new Afghan employee, Marla shuttled the women all over town and beyond. They visited schools, hospitals, microlending projects, and the World Food Program women's bakeries. They took a day trip to the Shomali Plain, north of Kabul. The frontline between the Northern Alliance militias and the Taliban had cut directly through the area. Once carpeted with vibrant farming villages, the plain had been pummeled to dust and ash. Refugees were slowly trickling back to their ruined homes with help from the United Nations, and teams of de-miners scoured the area for land mines. The women picnicked on a bluff overlooking the buckled plain. An hour's drive outside of Kabul, it had once been a popular weekend destination for families.

The pinnacle of the delegation's visit was International Women's Day, which was being celebrated at the new Ministry of Women's Affairs in Kabul. Following Marla and Bianca, the women entered the compound's mammoth front gates, which were guarded by truckloads of ragtag Afghan soldiers. Hundreds of people milled around a sprawling courtyard inside. Women with burkas flipped back over their heads chatted next to groups of female European soldiers smoking cigarettes. Marla and Bianca looked glamorous, with elegant scarves draped over their heads and shoulders. At one point, the president of Afghanistan, Hamid Karzai, strolled by in his own Afghan cap and cape, as did Mary Robinson, the former Irish prime minister and UN high commissioner for human rights at the time. Marla, Bianca, and the other delegates followed them into a VIP conference, during which Afghan women's rights were discussed for the first time in decades.

After the women returned home, Marla approached Sam Zia-Zarifi and congratulated him for sticking to the facts and not politicizing the issue. Over the next few weeks, Sam and Marla began talking more frequently. She shared her survey team's civilian casualty data with the Human Rights Watch researchers, and they reciprocated the favor.

Sam advised her, "You know, Marla, these guys aren't bad guys, and they'll just stop listening to you if you scream at them." Marla listened and nodded, but she wasn't ready to hang up her protester's hat just yet.

Chapter 7

Spring Fever

(How to Get Noticed by a Diplomat)

In Zimbabwe everyone's looking at Robert Mugabe, telling him how he should do things. So who is watching the Americans? It has to be us, the people.
—MARLA IN AN INTERVIEW WITH *NEWSWEEK*, APRIL 2002

By the time spring in Kabul was in full bloom, so was Marla. She was the centerpiece of every party. If she wasn't hosting a bash at her latest home, she was at the top of every guest list. But it was during daylight hours when Marla truly began to shine, and her brightest moment came on April 7.

Marla stood near Amina. The little girl was crouched in front of the fortified walls protecting the U.S. Embassy, holding her father Juma Khan's hand. The cobbler had borrowed money for the journey from their village in eastern Afghanistan to Kabul. He hoped the investment would pay off.

On a wintry November day, the family had been huddled over a meal when Amina got up from the carpet to fetch more tea in the kitchen. As the eight-year-old boiled water, the sky thundered overhead and bombs rained down onto Khanabad and onto their small home. Amina crawled out from under a heap of rubble unharmed and ran for help. Neighbors rushed to her aid and quickly freed Juma Khan from the debris. They continued digging—in vain. Juma Khan's wife, their seven other children, his mother, and his brother's family had all been killed. Eighteen relatives had sat down to break bread just moments before. By the time the warplanes vanished over the mountains, only two were alive.

With Marla at the helm, Amina and her father, along with about sixty other Afghans with equally haunting tales of loss, were asking the United States to pay for their mistakes.

April 7 was the six-month anniversary of Operation Enduring Freedom. To commemorate the beginning of the U.S. bombing raids, Marla and Ahmad arranged for the victims, some of whom were limping and blinded, to congregate at the embassy. The anniversary would give journalists a strong story about civilian casualties of war, and they were sure to turn out in force, which they did.

The real picture of nationwide civilian casualties remained murky; Marla still estimated that there had been two thousand deaths, but they hadn't documented nearly that many. Defying the odds, her survey teams had, however, made significant headway by April, locating scores of aggrieved families. Marla and Ahmad helped compose four hundred compensation petitions—for each injury, death, and destroyed home—to hand over to the Americans. Almost every person had not lost one or two relatives, but several.

Some lived in Kabul, while many others, like Amina, had traveled from their homes in eastern provinces where the United States and its allies had pursued al-Qaeda and the Taliban. Now they milled around in front of the embassy as Marla addressed the crowd from a concrete block, her hair exposed as usual. She roused some victims with her fiery display of indignation. Others watched on wearily, defeated. The journalists were listening, too. Reporters from some of America's top news dailies and weeklies showed up. Marla had become friendly with them during her tireless socializing and convinced them to come.

"It's been six months—it's too long," she told journalists. "We are saying each family should be compensated more or less ten thousand dollars to rebuild their home, to provide economic and welfare programs for women who can't work and whose husbands have died. . . . If there were two thousand families that were impacted, that's twenty million dollars—that's nothing. . . . There's no reason why they can say no to the compensation claims. It's the right thing to do!"

Someone else was finally listening. Michael Metrinko, the head of the embassy's political and consular sections, emerged from the building and exited the gates. Amina handed him a bulky folder containing sixteen death claims. The official, who speaks the Afghan Dari language, patiently listened to the Afghan victims. He was visibly moved by their tragic stories, but the embassy had been accepting the Global Exchange–facilitated claims since January, he told journalists, and he had asked Washington how to handle the matter.

Yet Marla wasn't satisfied. She pointed to Amina and seethed, "I have Amina here, who lost sixteen members of her family! What are you doing to help her?"

The following day, the *New York Times* ran a thousand-word article about the event in which Marla was quoted, and *Newsweek* wrote that she had "arguably become the best-known foreign figure in Kabul." Whether the embassy liked it or not, Marla had also become a force to be reckoned with.

Meanwhile, Medea was busy lobbying back in the United States. Joined by September 11 delegate and Peaceful Tomorrows cofounder Kelly Campbell, and Masuda Sultan, an Afghan-American woman whose relatives were killed in the U.S. bombing raids, she was scouring Washington for congressional allies to sponsor legislation that would require the U.S. government to compensate civilian victims. They were getting some promising nibbles, but nothing had come through yet. The women took advantage of their time in Washington to meet with as many influential people as possible. The Department of Defense refused to speak with them, but they managed to push through the State Department's doors for the first time in April 2002, and again in the summer. They were told that Marla's protests had created a public relations nightmare. Instead of being addressed, the issue of civilian casualties in Afghanistan had been buried under layers of bureaucracy and, in the end, relegated to damage control.

In March and April, Kabul's party scene was thriving, rotating from one Western compound to the next. The most decadent of the springtime bacchanals was hosted by the French

Embassy. The ambassador was out of town, and Kabul's expatriate community went wild. Journalists, aid workers, and diplomats washed down creamy pâté with French wine. Sam Zia-Zarifi of Human Rights Watch was there. So was Catherine Philp, a Scot in her early thirties writing for the *Times* of London. The fireplace roared, and a DJ spun Western tunes that pumped through the building's sound system. Marla and her new best friend, Bay Fang, a *U.S. News & World Report* correspondent, playfully wrapped their veils around each other as they bounced to the music like high school girls. The embassy had turned into a discotheque.

The mood in Kabul had lightened, but breaking curfew could still be hazardous. Journeying through town after hours required knowledge of the Northern Alliance militiamen's secret password. It changed daily, and some of the better-connected news agencies like CNN possessed the life-saving code, usually the name of a weapon followed by a set of numbers.

When she was through dancing at the French Embassy, Marla decided to host an after-party at Handicap International's house, where she was staying. Bay and Marla squeezed into a car full of foreigners and sped off into the pitch-black streets. Gangs of armed men awaited the curfew breakers at Kabul's various roundabouts and other checkpoints. They pointed Kalashnikovs at the vehicle's headlights and yelled menacingly for its driver to stop. Rolling down the window, the driver whispered the password of the day and was free to continue driving—until the next roundabout, when the whole routine was repeated.

* * *

By this time, Marla had added me to her swelling ranks of Kabul friends. The United Nations press conferences had shifted from the Intercontinental to the more central UN headquarters in town, where Marla often showed up with a stack of hand-scrawled party flyers. Like everyone else, I couldn't tell if she was for real or not. She didn't speak coherently about her work, jumping to more frivolous topics instead. Marla was a welcome relief from the packs of self-important and unsmiling UN employees I worked with during the day. She lit up a room with her childlike warmth. Although I was still perplexed by her purpose in Kabul, it was clear to me that she was the town's resident party girl, and I was grateful that she was plugging me into the circuit. I lunged at each invitation, craving an escape from the World Food Program's grim offices, where I slept in a cold room on a filthy mattress.

One night, she asked me over to dinner at the CBS News house. I arrived to a sumptuous spread of food set out on a long dining table. The CBS soundman, Massimo Casseriani, did double shifts as the house's gourmet chef. He invented a dish called the Marla Salad, which included pomegranate seeds and Parmesan cheese, preparing it whenever she requested, carefully soaking *souk*-bought tomatoes and cucumbers in a solution for an hour to kill any germs. Along with the Marla Salad, there was pasta with fresh sauce and a small ration of wine. Marla was clearly the hostess of the house but, I soon found out, one who didn't even live there.

CBS and ABC News divided the rambling space, and at

the time, Marla was having a fling with a British ABC producer. Whether he was there or not, she popped into the CBS side for Massimo's meals, inviting whomever she liked, creating a festive atmosphere for the male journalists. They gave Kabul's roving hostess whatever she wanted, including use of their Internet connection and satellite phones.

In April, the *Washington Post*'s Kabul bureau chief, Pam Constable, threw an elaborate party at the house to celebrate her fiftieth birthday. Pam, who was first astounded by Marla's sudden appearance at her dinner table in Jalalabad, had come to realize there was more to her than first met the eye. She'd seen Marla dozens of times around Kabul and remembered her as a "chic young elf" always dressed in flowery "California hippie" outfits that usually included jeans and a head veil.

Pam said that Marla reminded her of the young American idealists she'd met in El Salvador and Nicaragua in the 1980s. The human rights activists were mockingly known as "sandalistas." Pam recognized, however, a determined agenda behind Marla's carefree persona.

I'd never met Pam, but Marla invited me to her birthday celebration anyway. Knowing very few people outside of the UN in Kabul, I tentatively entered the house with a colleague. The back doors opened onto an expansive yard, where journalists were mingling in the spring night air. My friend was busy talking with an acquaintance, so I wandered out onto the lawn looking for a familiar face amongst the guests. All of a sudden I heard someone squealing, *"Jeeennnnnn!"*

I turned around and saw Marla prancing in my direction from the house, her arms outstretched for a hug. Unfortunately, there was a flower bed between us, containing what appeared to be tall rosebushes. Either Marla didn't see them or didn't care. She plowed straight into the foliage and tripped, disappearing beneath the thorny canopy. Before I could help, she sprang back up, squealing and laughing. I stared in astonishment. She continued on undeterred, the bandanna on her head slightly askew, and threw her arms around me as if she'd never been so delighted to see someone in her life. We chatted for a bit, and Marla gushed about how wonderful and beautiful I was. In a flash, she was off to embrace someone else who was wonderful and beautiful.

Marla had shoved a flyer for the "Prom" party into my hands before I hit the stage at one of the UN press briefings, and I held on to it. She was now living at the Wazir Akbar Khan house shared by National Public Radio and Voice of America, which would be the venue of the spring ball. For those who were present, it was certainly one of the more memorable nights in Kabul.

Marla happened to be just inside the door when I arrived. "Jen, you're here! Oh my *God*, there are, like, ten guys here who want . . . you!" Marla announced gleefully and far too loudly. I felt my cheeks turning red as several men grinned at me. I was shocked she'd made such a brazen announcement and doubted its veracity. I didn't know then that every thought that popped into her head maniacally bubbled out of her head unfiltered.

I moved into the living room. The place was packed. Men holding plastic cups lined the walls. A few brave souls started dancing in the living room between a couch and a small boom box. The lights were dimmed, and something hanging from the ceiling sparkled. Marla, Bay, and NPR correspondent Ivan Watson were decked out in 1970s formal wear they'd fished out of a Kabul thrift store. Marla teetered on black foam sandals in a slinky minidress that shimmered.

A couple of hours after the Prom's kickoff, Marla dragged herself off the dance floor and circulated with a wool Afghan hat she used for collecting donations. Marla now embodied Club Kabul.

Halfway through the night, Marla sobbed on a journalist's shoulder. She felt inadequate and that she wasn't doing all she could to help the Afghan families. Giving out ten dollars here and there wasn't good enough, she wept. After drying her eyes, she was back to twirling and giggling on the living room floor, as if nothing had happened. Her emotional outburst reminded those who saw it that tragedy lurked outside the prom's protective walls.

At around ten p.m., I realized I'd missed my curfew. A UN security officer was still there. I figured I'd catch a ride home with him later and moved onto a concrete deck in the backyard. Marla and Bay were sitting on a large chair, in front of where a street photographer had set up his boxy, old-fashioned camera kit on the deck. As they pouted suggestively at the camera, the photographer ducked under his black curtain to take their Prom portrait.

Things had begun to get a bit out of hand. Several

wide-eyed Afghan men crashed the party, and many were gaping at Marla and Bay. One of the world's most experienced foreign correspondents, Jon Lee Anderson of the *New Yorker* magazine, was concerned. In a space of a few months Afghans went from praying five times a day to drinking and watching girls in miniskirts dance. The young Westerners appeared oblivious to the cultural collision.

Marla yanked Jon Lee onto the dance floor when a Latin tune came on, temporarily breaking his observer's spell. She wanted to be twirled and he obliged, but her hand slipped from his grasp. She went flying onto the floor where she stayed, drunk, and unable to get up. He bent over and pulled Marla back onto her wobbly feet.

After curfew, Marla ushered me out the door with a pair of young *Newsweek* reporters. My ride had disappeared, so I threw caution to the wind. We were going to the reporters' house a few blocks away, she informed me, and I dutifully followed. A British newspaperman I knew was also stranded at the Prom without a ride home, so I invited him along. The five of us began walking down the middle of a very dark, very empty street. I didn't know the password but hoped someone did, suspecting this could be a potentially dangerous situation. My British friend obviously agreed and was whimpering by my side. Marla and the others assured me it was unlikely we'd run into any of the militias, as we weren't going far.

A few minutes later two headlights began rushing toward us. My instinct was to jump into the bushes. Marla, on the other hand, strutted ahead confidently in her thick-wedged heels. The minivan screeched to a stop and the side door slid open. I wasn't sure who the vehicle belonged to, but the Afghan driver seemed to know her. We all piled in for the short drive. When we safely reached the *Newsweek* house, I tumbled out with my three male companions. Before I noticed she wasn't with us, the car sped off with Marla still inside. I watched the minivan round the corner into the night.

Marla finally had a chance to become better acquainted with Jimin Lai, the AFP photographer she'd exchanged glances with in early 2002. They had kept in touch, and she booked a ticket to Malaysia to visit him. Jimin showed Marla some of the finer points of his home country, island-hopping and swimming in the warm sea. Although the relationship wouldn't continue any further, she was glowing after the rendezvous.

I happened to be in Islamabad when Marla was passing through town on her way back from Malaysia to Afghanistan later that spring. She crashed at my place and gave me a magenta silk scarf as thanks. My apartment was a five-minute walk from the Marriott Hotel, so we decided to head over one steamy afternoon.

Marla darted around the perimeter of the hotel's rectangular pool to cheerily greet friends. She stripped down to a bikini. Her body was tanned and lithe. I was struck by how thin she was; she was always hidden beneath her fur-collared Afghan vest in Kabul. Marla dived into the chlorinated water and smoothly churned an expert freestyle, leaving others splashing in her wake.

My job in the region was coming to a quick end; I would

be returning to the United States soon. Before parting ways, Marla and I consulted our schedules. It turned out we both expected to be in San Francisco in July. Making tentative plans to meet up for a drink in the Mission District, we said our good-byes.

It took me a while to find Baobab, a Senegalese restaurant named after a common African tree, just off Mission Street in San Francisco. The evening's event was already under way, and I quietly slipped into the back of the dining room. Marla pitched the night as a welcome home party, but in actuality, it was another fund-raiser.

"Hey, everybody, my friend Jen who worked for the World Food Program in Afghanistan is here too," Marla said, interrupting her presentation to point in my direction.

I gave a sheepish wave to the audience. A sea of heads turned toward me, then swiveled back to Marla in rapt attention. She held up large photographs of Afghan war victims, many of them children, and recounted their stories of loss in simple, engaging terms. She spoke slowly and clearly, and I was surprised. I knew her only from social settings, when she chattered like a ditzy teenager.

Marla finished her talk by announcing she had a pile of Pakistani and Afghan scarves for sale, whose proceeds would benefit the Afghan families.

After Marla's presentation, I talked with a couple of young attendees who bestowed a worshipful tone on me for my contribution to the people of Afghanistan. I tried to explain to them that the situation in Afghanistan was very complex and that, contrary to what they might think, not all Afghans hated America, and in fact, many were happy to be rid of the Taliban. I received blank, confused stares.

Once offstage, Marla was busy networking the Baobab crowd, but after a while, we found a moment to chat over drinks.

She was already fairly tipsy, and the conversation flipped from problems she was having with a prominent Green Party member who had broken her heart to frustration with the Global Exchange and San Francisco mentality. She was going to return to Afghanistan, but first she wanted to make a quick trip to Washington for some lobbying. The news had just come through that Haji Qadeer, the warlord and governor whose Jalalabad guesthouse she'd stayed in, had been assassinated in Kabul, where he had been serving as a vice president in Hamid Karzai's government. She was devastated and ached to be back in Afghanistan.

"I'm going to start my own organization!" she blurted.

I wished her luck, but doubted she could actually pull it off. I wouldn't see her again for nearly two years. In the time that passed, I discovered just how wrong I had been that night at Baobab.

Chapter 8

Frontline USA

(How to Change Foreign Policy)

*Babe, I was going to beat up that stupid lady who said some-
thing bad about you. But something that is so great about you
is even when people are lame you are still nice to them and
you don't spend time focusing on the bad stuff—[Your col-
league] said he would help me brainstorm some funding
[ideas] cause he was 25 when he started his first group too.*
—MARLA IN AN E-MAIL TO HER FRIEND AND
CNN TERRORISM ANALYST PETER BERGEN, AUGUST 2, 2002

Traveling with a small suitcase and a head
filled with ideas, Marla arrived in Washington, D.C., for
some fast-track networking. Her aim was to make a quick
reconnaissance mission to scope out ways to start her own
organization before returning to Afghanistan, where she
would give the victims' compensation claims one last push at
the embassy. The few sundresses she packed for the short
trip got a lot of mileage.

Marla's first stop in Washington was the home of Michael Shellenberger, the former Global Exchange reality tour guide who escorted her to Guatemala and Nicaragua in high school. Michael and his girlfriend at the time offered Marla a place on their couch for a few days, and in return, she gave them a woven piece of decorative Afghan fabric. Michael and Marla caught up. She gushed about how "amazing" the Afghan people were, and that she wanted to find a way to help them.

Michael suggested she speak with an acquaintance, Bobby Muller, the chairman of the Washington-based Vietnam Veterans of America Foundation (VVAF). Bobby had founded Vietnam Veterans of America (VVA), whose mandate was to fight for the rights of former U.S. soldiers, in 1978. VVAF evolved as an outgrowth of the organization and eventually broke off into a separate entity focusing on innocent victims of war, starting with Cambodia, where countless civilians had been maimed and killed by land mines. After Bobby traveled to the country with other Vietnam War veterans, his group began assisting Cambodian amputees and eventually became one of the founders of a worldwide campaign to prohibit the use of the indiscriminate explosives. More than 145 countries have signed an international agreement banning land mines, and the campaign won the Nobel Peace Prize in 1997. Marla picked up the phone without hesitation.

A few hours later she was in Bobby's office, chattering effusively. His dark eyes inspect your own when he talks. He has a head of neatly cropped white hair and speaks with a strong Long Island accent. Bobby has also been confined to a wheelchair since 1969. A bullet pierced his chest and snapped his spinal cord while he was on active duty in Vietnam. Marla wasn't exactly the kind of person he was used to seeing on the premises. Still despite her California lingo, what she was saying blew him away. Her passion to help civilian war victims mirrored his own.

"What can I do to help the Afghan victims? How do I do what you've done?" she asked him.

Bobby knew just the man to call.

Tim Rieser has been described by friends as the "Conscience of the Senate." He has worked for Senator Patrick Leahy, a Democrat from Vermont, for more than twenty years. Since 1989 Tim has been Leahy's indispensable aide on the Foreign Operations Subcommittee for the U.S. Senate Committee on Appropriations. Leahy, a past chairman, now serves as its ranking minority member. The office decides how taxpayer money is spent overseas, excluding U.S. military deployment. Its annual budget is roughly thirty billion dollars. It funds the cost of everything from the United Nations and the World Bank to smaller humanitarian projects administered by the United States Agency for International Development (USAID) in countries like Afghanistan. Senator Leahy has been a staunch proponent of human rights and programs assisting victims of war throughout his long incumbency. Tim, a lawyer and Vermont native, has been Leahy's key staffer on the committee from the get-go. If any group or individual needs a sponsor to support legislation of a socially conscious nature, they often lobby Senator Leahy through Tim. Talking with him is especially important for anyone trying to squeeze a few dollars out of the annual foreign appropriations budget.

Bobby Muller had worked with Tim on the land mine campaign and against the death penalty. They were old friends, so while Marla was in his office, Bobby called to ask Tim to dinner, promising they would be joined by someone worth meeting.

Tim was running late that night after another long day at the Senate. Bobby and Marla were already seated at McCormick and Schmick's restaurant on K Street, Washington's lobbyist row, when he arrived. Wafer-thin, with wispy salt-and-pepper hair, Tim was dressed neatly in jeans and a button-up shirt. He sat down with his friend and the unknown blonde, who looked no more than a girl. Over the course of their meal, Tim realized he had seen Marla's name in the *New York Times* after the April 7 embassy protest. He was impressed by her work, but he was also skeptical about her chances at winning financial compensation for civilian victims of U.S. warfare.

Tim had tried unsuccessfully to get compensation after the invasion of Panama that resulted in the capture of Noriega. Several hundred people living in a shantytown next to General Noriega's palace died when the area burned as a result of U.S. bombs in 1989. A group of lawyers seeking compensation for these families got hold of Tim's number and called him. The Appropriations Defense Subcommittee and the Pentagon were absolutely adamant that they were not going to give compensation to innocent civilians, presumably fearing the precedent it might set and that they would then be expected to help anyone who was a casualty of war.

The dinner with Bobby Muller and Tim Rieser resulted in a series of meetings in government conference rooms before Marla returned to Afghanistan, delaying her trip indefinitely. She realized that she would have much more luck finding assistance for war victims by speaking calmly inside the Senate, especially with Tim's help, than screaming outside the embassy in Kabul.

Marla's survey team had collected an abundance of data in Afghanistan, but she had yet to patch the information together into the "Portraits of Grief" report. Medea was pressuring her to complete it for mass distribution to the investors and media. But as usual, Marla's nature propelled her headlong into action rather than concentrating on more cerebral projects. She was in a prime position to push the issue of compensation in Washington circles, and time was of the essence. In a way, Marla didn't need a paper to prove her point. She possessed a collection of case studies, including real, human accounts and photographs of the victims, their surviving family members, and their destroyed homes. Also, the stories were fresh in her mind. She had personally sat in many modest homes holding the hands of wailing Afghans and hugging their children. For immediate lobbying purposes, she *was* the report, made of flesh and blood and a fair amount of California charisma.

Omar Samad, the Afghan Foreign Ministry spokesman who Marla knew from Kabul, was in town. He invited her to accompany him to Perry's, in the trendy Adams Morgan neighborhood. The second-story restaurant has a quaint rooftop terrace, replete with a bar perfect for summer sundowners.

The pair entered and couldn't have been more mismatched. Omar, a classic diplomat, glided in with debonair grace while Marla twittered at his side. They were joining Omar's old pal Peter Bergen, who is CNN's terrorism analyst and author of the seminal book about the al-Qaeda network, *Holy War, Inc.* As it was a warm evening, the three climbed the stairs to the roof.

"Peter, I've heard so much about you and how great you are!" Marla gushed unabashedly as they greeted each other. He took to her immediately.

Peter speaks with a British accent and wears his hair in a typically English floppy style. Although he was educated in the UK, he actually hails from Minnesota. His authoritative television voice contrasts a more affable off-camera personality, which is punctuated by energetic spurts of intense emotion and goofy giggles—kind of like Marla.

The evening with Omar would be the first of many that Marla and Peter would spend together at Perry's, often joined by his boisterous and accomplished clique of Washington friends. She had decided to stay on indefinitely to work with Tim in an effort to win her Afghan families some government assistance—and possibly to start her own organization. Impressed by her ambitions, Peter immediately invited her to crash at his townhouse. Resplendent with ornate Afghan rugs, it is in the upscale Dupont Circle neighborhood. He shares the space with his seventy-five-year-old father. Marla kept the older man company despite her manic life, taking him on regular coffee outings to a nearby Starbucks.

Peter initiated Marla into the Washington scene, and she instantly bonded with several people, including Shaun Waterman, a British United Press International reporter, and Nicole Boxer, a documentary filmmaker who is also the daughter of California Democratic senator Barbara Boxer. Instead of talking politics, Marla and Nicole gossiped about their relationships and other girlish topics on their frequent visits to the steam bath at the gym. Within a very short space of time, Marla became as well known as Peter in Washington.

She was hard at work the whole time, bouncing between VVAF, where Bobby offered her a free desk, and Tim's Senate offices. Their goal was to persuade various Washington officials that assisting civilians inadvertently harmed by U.S. warfare would benefit, rather than damage, the nation. It was the right thing to do—as policy. The delicate negotiation process was like walking a tightrope—any misstep could lead to a fall. Marla's fiery temper needed taming.

The first step of the negotiation process began immediately. Tim and Senator Leahy rushed to insert language into an upcoming supplemental appropriations bill that would provide government funds to assist civilian communities affected by military action in Afghanistan.

Tim recognized a gold mine in Marla. Any doubts he had about her credibility vanished when she came to his office one day with Kelly Cambell of Peaceful Tomorrows. Reassured, he was hopeful that Marla's personal experience might help convince officials at the State Department and Pentagon, who could easily block precedent-setting legislation, to support Afghan victims of war. If she learned to speak in politically neutral language, who would be able to ignore her stories about wounded and orphaned children?

From the day their collaboration began, Tim tirelessly coached Marla on presentation. He taught her how to talk to Washington bureaucrats in a way they could understand. Tim helped Marla metamorphose from a San Francisco leftist into a human rights advocate whom Washington would take seriously. She was a very willing subject and caught on quickly.

Marla and Tim often walked clear across Washington to his Senate offices. It gave them plenty of time to talk.

"How do we get the compensation to the right victims who were bombed?" Marla asked one day.

"Nobody will listen to you if you say 'compensation.' We need to find a way to get 'assistance' to victims of the 'accidental' bombings," Tim corrected.

Marla spent hours brainstorming in Tim's office. To save time, she'd often Rollerblade to the Senate, gliding across the lobby's glistening stone floors—and past bewildered men in dark suits.

That summer Secretary of Defense Donald Rumsfeld and General Tommy Franks, who then directed the war, testified during a hearing about the military's activities in Afghanistan. Marla took a seat in the Dirksen Senate Office Building to listen, hoping they would discuss the issue of civilian casualties of war. They did not. Disappointed, Marla marched right up to them after the hearing. She had just come from Afghanistan, she said, where harmed and grieving civilians needed assistance. Talking the whole time, Marla accompanied Rumsfeld out of the hearing room, down the hallway, and onto the curb, where his driver was waiting. Marla handed Rumsfeld some of her Afghan survey information just before he ducked into the car, then watched as he disappeared down the road and into traffic.

Whether or not Rumsfeld ever read the materials, an unprecedented triumph for civilian victims was on the horizon. Just a few days later, with Tim and Marla's help, Senator Leahy won the needed support to include language in a supplemental appropriations bill requiring that funds be made available in fiscal year 2002 to repair Afghan homes that were damaged by U.S. bombs. As ordered by U.S. law, USAID would grant $1.5 million to a relief agency working on the ground in Afghanistan. It was mere pennies relative to the overall appropriations budget, but in symbolic terms, the legislation was priceless. The law, which specifically provided assistance for noncombatant victims accidentally harmed by U.S. warfare, was enacted on August 2, 2002.

It was the first of its kind in American history.

Things were looking up for Marla in D.C. Bay Fang, her friend from Kabul, was moving to town; she had joined a Girls Night Out club whose members were primarily thirty-something Washington movers and shakers; assistance for some Afghan victims seemed to be imminent; and she was adding fresh contacts to her Rolodex every day. But she couldn't stay still in Washington, and traveled every few weeks over the course of the next six months.

In mid-August she zipped up to New York, where she hunted down Sam Zia-Zarifi at Human Rights Watch's headquarters. Reiterating how much she respected the group's professional approach to their research, Marla indicated that she wanted to keep collaborating with the organization. Next she flew to California.

After a quick chill-out session in San Francisco and Lakeport, she shed her bikini and headed back to D.C. and Capitol Hill. Surrounded by policy makers, her head was abuzz with a swarm of ideas. Marla plied her new Washington friends with the same intense adulation as she did in college and Kabul.

Just before the one-year anniversary of September 11, Marla took a quick trip to Afghanistan. She would try to help her families apply for the U.S. aid that Senator Leahy had secured.

After tying up loose ends, she reluctantly left. The assistance hadn't begun yet, and she was needed in Washington, so she rented a postage stamp apartment on 19th Street behind the Hilton Hotel near Adams Morgan. Her mom, Nancy, flew out to help her. Everything seemed to be in place, yet she began to feel overwhelmed and neglected her own well-being.

September did not end quietly in Washington, D.C. The final three days of the month began with anti–World Bank and International Monetary Fund demonstrations and ended with a march to Vice President Dick Cheney's residence, protesting an Iraq invasion. Marla joined the protesters who streamed through the capital, but her professional focus remained fixed on Capitol Hill. A little over a week later, she received a phone call that put everything on hold.

Phillip woke up at five a.m. on October 7, 2002, with blood streaming down his face. The nosebleed didn't stop for five hours. He went to the emergency room, where the bleeding was contained. The next day, the same thing occurred, and this time, the doctors suggested he make an appointment with his general practitioner for some blood tests. When the results came in, he was rushed back to the emergency room. His blood cell count—white, red, and platelets—was dangerously low. After more tests and several biopsies, the doctors found that his bone marrow stem cell count was at 5 percent, much lower than the normal 70 percent. Phillip was admitted to the hospital. There were three explanations for his illness, some better than others. At best, he was suffering from an acute vitamin B-12 deficiency. At worst, leukemia. The third possibility was a rare immunodeficiency disease called aplastic anemia that normally strikes children and young adults.

Marla rushed from Washington to his bedside in California while he awaited the final diagnosis. Although she and Phillip had gone their separate ways, they remained extremely close, talking regularly on the phone while she was in Afghanistan. Now it was her turn to do the worrying. He looked and felt normal, but his blood count kept sliding to increasingly life-threatening levels.

The verdict came in the following day. Phillip was diagnosed with aplastic anemia. The good news was that it wasn't leukemia, but he still faced a long and shaky road to recovery. The invasive treatment could last indefinitely—if he survived.

War in Iraq was fast changing from "if" to "when." Although it was painful leaving Phillip, Marla returned to Washington to get back to work. On October 11, Congress passed the Authorization for Use of Military Force Against Iraq Resolution of 2002, giving the president the green light to attack if Saddam did not give up weapons of mass destruction, or WMDs. Marla already knew where she would be heading next.

As the war drums grew louder, she gradually reset her sights from Kabul to Baghdad. No longer working for Global Exchange, she wanted, at the very least, to have the name and logo of an organization emblazoned onto a stack of business cards before she went to Iraq. Bobby was now paying her as a full-time consultant, so she could continue her civilian casualties lobbying in Washington and focus on building her own nonprofit. Not everyone at VVAF was ecstatic about Marla. Some straitlaced Washingtonians were perplexed by the appearance of a ditzy blonde on their premises, and they viewed her with some derision. Marla's tendency to party a bit too much in a city where people run in very tight circles didn't help her image. Also, according to some people, there were jealousies.

Marla stayed as a consultant on and off for about a year, bouncing into the office whenever she returned from another trip. Bobby eventually had to let her go due to "changes" in the organization. So he began supporting her from his own pocket by depositing money directly into her personal bank account. In those early months, Bobby vigilantly tutored his new consultant in his offices. He let Marla in on the secrets of his own success in Washington, such as making sure to moderate rhetoric, remaining bipartisan, and matching lobbyists to politicians by party affiliation.

One activist who disapproved of Marla's work with the government was Medea. Marla was no longer taking an antiwar stance in her work. Her job was to help civilians and she needed the U.S. government to do so. It became clear that Marla had slipped from the activist community's grasp.

In the end, Marla never finished "Portraits of Grief"; she was too busy working with Tim on the appropriations legislation. Frustrated with her lack of delivery, Global Exchange finally put another employee in charge of piecing the surveys together into narrative form.

The report is impressive. It cites that Marla's five-member survey team documented 824 civilian deaths resulting from U.S. warfare in Afghanistan between October 2001 and January 2002. It also acknowledges that they were unable to determine an accurate total number of civilians killed, due to ongoing warfare and inaccessibility to many Afghan regions and provinces. Bombings continued after the survey team completed its work in June 2002. One heavily publicized case took place in July, when bombs mistakenly struck a wedding party in the remote Uruzgan Province in central Afghanistan, killing an estimated fifty people and injuring a hundred more.

In its conclusion, the report recommended that the U.S. government conduct its own civilian casualty investigation and create the twenty-million-dollar "Afghan Victims Fund" that Marla referred to during her embassy protests. It also strongly suggested a ban on the use and manufacture of cluster bombs because of their potential for indiscriminate harm. The small, colorful bombs frequently fail to explode upon impact and often end up blowing off children's hands and arms.

Perhaps the most striking feature of "Portraits of Grief" is its human element. Like the *New York Times* obituaries of the September 11 victims, it attaches stories to the numbers of dead. It also exhibits photographs of injured children and grieving relatives whose lives were destroyed by the U.S. bombing. It opens with a touching account by Masuda Sultan, the young Afghan-American woman who worked with Medea and Kelly lobbying for an Afghan Victims Fund on Capitol Hill. Two months before the bombing campaign began, Masuda traveled to Afghanistan for the first time since she was five to meet her extended family. After the commencement of the war, she returned to look for them, eventually finding a few distraught relatives in a Pakistani refugee camp. They told her that one pregnant cousin was sliced in half on October 22, 2001, when the bombs began strafing her family's village near the Taliban's base of Kandahar in southern Afghanistan. A little girl was shot dead while fleeing the attack. In all, nineteen of her relatives were killed. None were affiliated with al-Qaeda or the Taliban.

Even if the survey's collective effort failed to deliver an accurate statistic, it did succeed in introducing the world to the human cost of the war in Afghanistan. Through the media, it was Marla's voice that implored American leaders to pay attention to the injured Afghans who stood next to her at the embassy. In Washington, with Tim and Bobby's help, she retold their stories, politely asking the government to do the same. The "Portraits of Grief" process was groundbreaking in that it did help change U.S. policy—even if it didn't fulfill its original goals of producing a complete tally of the dead or directly compensating victims.

In Afghanistan the enemy primarily hid in the country's sparsely populated backwoods. The focus of an Iraq bombing campaign and invasion, however, would be largely urban. Saddam's regime and army were bound to hole up amid the millions of civilians residing in Baghdad and other Iraqi cities. Experts predicted that the civilian death toll would be much higher in an Iraq showdown. With Senator Leahy at the helm, Tim and Marla were already gearing up to push through similar legislation for Iraqi civilians if Bush cried war.

The more Marla became entrenched in Washington, the more likely it seemed she would soon be yanked away. War in Iraq was looming. On November 9, the United Nations Security Council passed Resolution 1441, which offered Saddam Hussein one last chance to disarm his alleged stockpiles of WMDs or face "serious consequences." On November 27, the inspectors began their mission in Iraq.

Marla returned to California over Thanksgiving to hold a number of meetings and to check in on Phillip. His difficult treatment had begun, which rendered his immune system ineffectual. He was getting top-notch care at the

University of California Medical Center in San Francisco. She tried to stay optimistic.

The doctors said that Phillip would probably pull through, but because he was vulnerable to infection, Marla had to wear a face mask when visiting him in the hospital. Any cough or sniffle could prove deadly. He was receiving regular blood transfusions, which sapped his strength. The sight of him in this condition made Marla hysterical.

Phillip wanted Marla there, but his energy levels were too low to comfort her. He told Marla that he wouldn't be angry if she left, assuring her that he would be fine. Although she was racked with guilt, Marla returned to Washington.

The constant moving around started to wear on her. During Peter Bergen's fortieth birthday party in mid-December, Peter had to take her back to her tiny apartment, where she collapsed in a drunken heap, one hour after the party began. Shortly after, Marla wrote an apologetic e-mail to him in which she came down hard on her own behavior, acknowledging that she was feeling lonely and overworked. She pushed on anyway, and even farther away from home.

Desert Storm

(How to Hitch a Ride to Baghdad)

I mean, the goal is to stop the war, but people are preparing in case there is a war!
—MARLA TALKING TO MEDEA BENJAMIN ON FILM
IN IRAQ, FEBRUARY 2003

Marla had one ambition: to find a way into Iraq. She was anxious to get a head start on assembling a civilian casualty survey team on the ground before the war began. In Afghanistan, the process began almost half a year after the first bombs exploded. By the time her small team of surveyors canvassed the country for data, hospital beds had been long vacated and the dead had been buried in the remote, barren wasteland for months. The experience of managing that tally taught her that the sooner she got started, the more likely she was to get an accurate count of the wounded and dead. The quicker she got this information to Tim and Senator Leahy, she thought, the quicker they could push through legislation providing assistance for Iraqi war victims.

In order to help her new friends and, in effect, the Iraqi civilians, Marla turned to her old comrades. She would use the peace activist card to get into Iraq. Baghdad heaved with foreign antiwar demonstrators who were flowing into Iraq unhindered. She could easily pass herself off as one of them. All she needed to do was slip back into her old skin for a few days.

Saddam Hussein's regime welcomed the foreigners to Iraq with open arms. His Committee of Friendship and Solidarity with the Peoples was happy to issue entry visas to the pierced, tattooed, and dreadlocked martyrs. The human shields were eager to shackle themselves to hospitals and schools to prevent the U.S. military from dropping bombs on them—even though such plans never existed. The Baath Party had its own plan in mind, and the foreigners unwittingly became pawns of the regime. They were shuttled to power stations and other strategic sites instead of places where children gathered. Saddam, who ordered the slaughter of thousands of his own countrymen, wasn't so interested in the welfare of Iraqi civilians. He wanted to maintain control of the country. The more civilians killed, the worse the United States would look.

Shortly after her arrival in mid-January, a group of German peace activists agreed to take Marla into Baghdad. On the quick reconnaissance mission, Marla ended up in Amman, Jordan, when her visa expired. She remained there until her next ride into Baghdad showed up—Medea and her CODEPINK peace delegation.

Medea had founded CODEPINK, a women's antiwar group, in November. Amman became Marla's on-and-off base for the next two months, and when she wasn't crashing with friends and acquaintances in their plush accommodations, she checked into a small, cheap hotel downtown. She attended press conferences and organized parties in the basement of one of Amman's opulent hotels, where all the journalists were staying. One hotel manager, Marla said, accused her of being a spy. Suspicious of the young American who wasn't attached to a media or humanitarian organization, he forbade her from entering the premises.

John Monte, a filmmaker documenting the CODEPINK delegation's trip to Iraq, captured footage of Marla before the war began. The tapes vividly expose the gaping fissure in Medea and Marla's surrogate mother-daughter relationship.

Marla was gesticulating wildly in her Afghan fur-collared vest. Her arms flapped for emphasis and she pounded the center of a flattened palm with the point of five pinched fingers from her other hand. A glaring blur of Iraqi highway whizzed past. Sitting next to an open window in the backseat, Marla was arguing with an invisible figure in the front of the car. Medea's disembodied voice was audible, and it did not like what Marla was saying.

"I mean, the goal is to stop the war, but people are preparing in case there is a war!"

Medea cut in, criticizing groups and people like herself setting up shop for a postconflict relief effort, instead of protesting the war.

"I'm not asking for career advice! I'm just saying I'm paying attention. I'm learning about it because it interests me. They're planning just in case!" Marla retorted, droning out Medea's words.

She continued arguing her point, defending a reputable

American NGO that was making preparations for the war.

"We didn't even invite her. She just came and used the delegation to get her visa and to come in with us," Medea later said.

Medea's disapproval didn't cloud Marla's newfound vision; she was convinced that her way was the right way and no longer wanted her old mentor telling her what to do. On a personal level, however, she was very hurt by Medea's negative reaction to her ambitions. Even if their present views diverged, they had been extremely close for many years. Medea was equally injured. It was clear that Marla had used the delegation to get into Iraq for her own purposes.

Marla left Iraq with the CODEPINK delegation after spending ten days with them. To her dismay, she wasn't able to get a visa extension. So it was back to Amman, then to Washington to make some last-minute preparations for a move to Iraq. She laid the groundwork for her own organization without completing the appropriate legal steps, such as filing paperwork with the Internal Revenue Service. She had a business card printed up, calling her one-woman show the Iraq Victims Compassion Campaign. A few months later, Marla would change the name of her organization to Campaign for Innocent Victims in Conflict, or CIVIC.

On her way to Amman from D.C. in early March 2003, Marla met up with Jon Swain at London's Heathrow airport. The older British *Sunday Times* correspondent hadn't been able to secure an Iraqi visa yet. He was traveling to Beirut, Lebanon, on assignment in the meantime. Crazy about Jon, Marla rerouted her ticket in a matter of moments.

Marla had first stayed with Jon back in January. She had been on her way to Amman, Jordan, where she'd try to find a way into Iraq, but stopped off in London for a few days first. She and Jon had kept in touch, and over the course of the next year, she stopped off in London when shuttling between Washington and Baghdad. During each visit, Jon and Marla spent two or three intense days having long discussions and dining at posh West London restaurants. In the mornings she strapped on a pair of Rollerblades and raced down London's leafy boulevards for her daily exercise regimen before rushing off to meet other friends. Jon has a daughter and a son, the products of two failed relationships. Half his age, Marla showered him with fathering tips.

Marla was completely enamored by Jon. She almost idolized him. However their views on the relationship were not synchronized: Jon saw Marla more as a cherished friend but continued to see her romantically anyway.

In Lebanon, Marla and Jon stayed at the Phoenicia, a luxury hotel overlooking the Mediterranean Sea. She enjoyed long swims and spent time in the gym during the day while he was working. In the evenings, they dined on seafood. She drank wine but held herself together. She was content being alone with Jon for four or five days, but she soon grew restless. Her mind swirled with new ideas. Strategies and plans for Iraq invaded her every thought. She left Jon and Beirut behind.

Back in Amman, Marla continued to crash press briefings, network, and socialize with journalists, letting everyone in on her plans. War was now palpable. U.S. and British troops had amassed in the region. The United

States and Britain were pressuring the UN Security Council to pass a second resolution sanctioning an attack. They faced fierce opposition from other members, notably France and Germany. The weapons inspectors requested more time to complete their work. Impatient, President Bush pushed ahead with plans despite the lack of a new Security Council resolution. He addressed the world on March 17, issuing Saddam Hussein and his two sons an ultimatum: Either leave Iraq within forty-eight hours, or prepare for an attack. The next day, the weapons inspectors abandoned their mission and fled the country. Saddam and his sons stayed put.

After finishing up his work in Beirut, Jon flew to Amman shortly after Marla. In order to get them both Iraqi tourist visas, she began working her contacts. In the meantime, Jon's visa miraculously came through with the help of another source. It was just in time. In the wee hours of the morning of March 20, the first allied bombs dropped on Iraq. The war had begun. Jon would drive straight through to Baghdad. Marla wanted to join him, but he didn't like the idea.

"What are you going to do? You're not going to be able to work. The city's going to be bombed. It's much more important to come afterward, and it's a bit irresponsible to come now. You're not campaigning against the war," Jon counseled her.

Because of his years of experience covering wars, she trusted his opinion. It was almost painful for her to stay behind, but she took Jon's advice. Instead, Marla visited the Jordanian relatives of the first known civilian casualty of the war in Iraq. The Jordanian taxi driver was killed by a bomb that plowed into his car as he was racing back to the safety of Amman.

Marla entered a room full of wailing men and women devastated by the news. They eyed the American girl through angry tears. She wore a pained, sympathetic expression on her own face, calmly listening to the relatives express their sorrow. Through a translator, she told them how sorry she was and asked if there was anything she could do to help them. She sat down on the family couch, placing her hand on top of that of a sobbing woman, gingerly collecting the needed information about their loved one's death. She was the only American offering an apology for their loss, taking on what should have been the responsibility of a U.S. government or military official.

One place Marla could go outside of Amman was Ruweished. Traveling there required a Jordanian government-issued permit, but it was easier to obtain than an Iraqi visa. Many journalists who were not embedded with U.S. troops dashed to the dusty Jordanian border town, hoping to push through into Iraq in the days before the bombing began. Marla spent a few days there too. Little more than a glorified truck stop with a few dreary houses in the background, Ruweished is a three-and-a-half-hour drive east from Amman through flat, rocky desert. It was normally worth visiting only to fill up on gas and stock up on food and water found in a handful of shops and kiosks before continuing on into Iraq, but in the weeks leading up to the war, some NGOs set up two refugee camps just outside of Ruweished in anticipation of receiving a flood of Iraqis escaping the looming war. Marla was sitting in the shade of a Bedouin tent near Ruweished with David Wright, an ABC News correspondent she knew from Kabul. She had run into David in Amman, where she told him about her recent success working with Senator Leahy to help war victims in Afghanistan and how they planned on doing the same for Iraqis. He was impressed with her transformation and smelled an interesting television story.

David pitched Marla's story to his bosses back in London and New York. They turned it down, fatigued with the abundance of Iraq war coverage. David was crestfallen.

The first signs of human loss were not as disastrous as many feared. Human Rights Watch reported that, as in Afghanistan, it appeared that the United States had taken precautions to avoid civilian casualties and that losses had been minimal relative to the scale of the firepower. The urban nature of the war had nonetheless trapped many ordinary Iraqis in the crossfire, as predicted. A British-based website called Iraq Body Count began posting a tally of the dead drawn from news reports citing specific incidents that killed civilians. The site claimed that between 212 and 292 civilians had been killed during the first week of hostilities. By late March, Marla was twitching in Amman. It was everything she could do to hold herself back from trying to sneak into Iraq where she could assess the situation herself. Remembering Jon's words, she resisted the temptation.

Baghdad was falling and fast. The U.S. Army's 3rd Infantry Division rumbled into the Iraqi capital on April 8 after a three-and-a-half week sweep northward from Kuwait. Their tanks rolled down major palm-lined roads next to the Tigris. They stopped at Saddam Hussein's New Presidential Palace and moved in. Along with the rest of the world, Marla stared in amazement at the television screen. On April 9 she watched images of an American tank drag to the ground the statue of Saddam Hussein in downtown Baghdad's Fardous Square, where a group of Iraqi men and boys whacked the bronze carcass with their shoes. The Iraqi border guards were likely to abandon their posts. Visas would be rendered obsolete and unnecessary with the Americans in charge, and no one wanted to be left behind. Seeing a window of opportunity, every journalist in Amman made a mad dash for Ruweished, hoping to move on to Iraq, in case U.S. soldiers soon sealed the border.

Marla latched onto three older female journalists who'd hired a driver and a GMC Suburban. She had tried to get them all tourist visas in Amman, but failed. They took pity on Marla, who was penniless as usual. Familiar with her work in Afghanistan, where they remembered her as "Bubbles" spinning in circles at the Prom party, they agreed to bring the much younger woman along with them. They arrived in Ruweished late at night, parking in a long line of other GMC Suburbans belonging to journalists.

The next morning, they wandered over to Abu Sayf, the more popular of two restaurants in town, to grab a cup of coffee and watch scenes of Baghdad on CNN. The dingy café was covered with business cards that had been pinned to the inside walls by journalists, aid workers, and political activists over the past ten years. Many new ones had been added that day. The place was packed with some hundred journalists dividing into cliques, all hatching schemes on how to cross over the border. Once the Iraqi guards fled, the Americans were bound to seal it off again. Marla was agitated. She paced back and forth, trying to contain an overwhelming sense of frustration. She chitchatted with friends but was distracted by the plans spinning in her head. She was wasting valuable work time. She had waited so long already, and every moment she wasn't in Baghdad represented a life she couldn't help. But there was nothing she could do to expedite her arrival; she was totally dependent on her companions, a *USA Today* reporter and two journalists working for the *Chicago Tribune*, who were carefully making the safest travel plans possible. The Iraqi border guards had indeed fled, and it seemed the Americans had not closed the gates. The convoy of GMCs would leave for Baghdad at dawn.

The women couldn't sleep. At four a.m. on April 11 they decided to cross the border on their own. They didn't want to be stuck in the conspicuous convoy and were concerned that the Americans would close the border by the time they reached the front of the line. There was a chill in the dry air. They pulled out from the line of cars and crept toward the border. As the sun came up, the landscape was eerily empty. An hour later, they reached the frontier and crossed under a broad archway. A young American soldier standing under a poster of Saddam Hussein smiled and waved them on. "Yay!" Marla chirped, clapping her hands.

Their initial elation was dampened when they reached a roadblock manned by American soldiers. After leaving Jordan, the highway to Baghdad slices through the desert in a northeast arc. As the road draws nearer to the capital, it cuts through the cities of Ramadi and Fallujah, which, the soldiers told them, were raging with fierce fighting. The soldiers suggested they take a detour south on a back road that meandered through an arid no-man's-land, finally looping north to Baghdad from the city of Karbala. They took a right turn, passing villages that looked as if they had been frozen in time two thousand years ago. An unbridled herd of camels galloped past them. After several hours weaving through the wild badlands, the women realized they were lost.

Marla's body was taut, and she looked out the window at nothing, again growing distressed. She wanted to be in Baghdad, now. She twisted her legs into a yoga position to relax. She turned quiet, crawled into the back of the Suburban, lodged herself between pieces of luggage and boxes of bottled water, and tried to sleep. The journalists were confused by the sudden change in her behavior.

The light began to fade, and cool night air swept over the desert. Their gas tank was dangerously low, and the journalists' nerves began to frazzle as well. Iraq was in a state of complete anarchy, with gunmen, bandits, and warfare, and they, three blondes and a redhead, were completely off the map without protection. They stopped on the side of the road, deciding to spend the night in the desert. The journalists were unpacking their satellite phones to alert friends and colleagues of their predicament when they noticed something on the horizon.

A young Marla with friends on Halloween in Lakeport
Courtesy of the McGuire Family

*A teenage Marla posing with her new
"protest-mobile" in Lakeport*
Courtesy of the McGuire Family

*Marla; her brother, Mark; and her parents, Cliff and
Nancy, during Marla's college graduation party at the
Ruzicka family home, June 1999*
Wilford Low

Marla and Phillip Machingura in Vilanculos, Mozambique, May 1999
Courtesy of Phillip Machingura

Marla and Phillip Machingura on their wedding day at San Francisco's City Hall, March 27, 2000
Courtesy of Phillip Machingura

Marla protesting during an Enron meeting at the Commonwealth Club in San Francisco, 2001
San Francisco Chronicle/Kate Wade

Marla protesting in front of the U.S. Embassy in Kabul, April 7, 2002
The Daily Telegraph/Heathcliff O'Malley

Marla in Kabul in early 2002
Kate Brooks

Marla dancing with a friend and Quil Lawrence (right) at the Mustafa Hotel in Kabul, January 2002
Rick Loomis

Marla waving from the backseat of a taxicab in Kabul, January 2002
Rick Loomis

Marla posing amid the ruins of Kabul, early 2002
Kate Brooks

Marla holding a young Iraqi girl
Courtesy of CIVIC

(below) *The last photograph taken of Marla, in Baghdad with Zahra's sister and grandmother, April 15, 200*
World Picture News/Scott Nelso

arla's pallbearers preparing to escort her casket into the church at her funeral service in Lakeport, April 23, 2005
casket, left to right: Julie Pyzer, Peter Bergen, Colby Smart, Quil Lawrence, Catherine Philp. In foreground: Bobby Muller.
ress Democrat/Kent Porter

Marla's parents, Cliff and Nancy Ruzicka, at their daughter's funeral reception in Lakeport on April 23, 2005
Press Democrat/Kent Porter

Marla's friends from Kabul and Baghdad at her funeral reception in Lakeport on April 23, 2005
Front Row: Jack Fairweather and Christina Asquith, first and second from the left; Adam Davidson, Jen Banbury, and author
Jennifer Abrahamson, first, second, and third from the right. Middle Row: Patrick Graham, Tara Sutton, Kate Brooks, Chris
Hondros, and Catherine Philp, from left to right. Back Row: Jon Lee Anderson and Rick Loomis, second and fourth from the lef
Courtesy of Chris Hondros

Marla Ruzicka
1976-2005
Courtesy of CIVIC

Squinting, they made out a tank about a third of a mile away. A soldier was perched at its gun turret. The women began jumping up and down, frantically waving their arms.

"We're American! We're American! Please help us!" they shouted.

The soldier thought he had glimpsed a mirage. He rolled his machine over to the women. Soldiers spilled out of the tank and stared, their bearded jaws hanging open. They hadn't seen a Western woman for some time.

They were nowhere near Baghdad. Instead, they were skirting the Saudi Arabian border in a deeply Sunni tribal area. Their Jordanian driver had taken a wrong turn, veering them far off course. The journalists explained to the soldiers that they were trying to get to Baghdad and were running on empty. Marla hovered behind her companions.

The soldiers turned their backs to the women and ducked into a huddle. After a few minutes, the men returned. They were still edgy in those first days after victory and were concerned about security, but nonetheless said the women were welcome to spend the night at their camp. More than a safe haven, the journalists had stumbled onto an exclusive story. It turned out that the soldiers were Special Forces. The highly specialized combat veterans had been holed up in an abandoned house in the nearby village of Nukhayb for several weeks, emerging only the day before when the tank arrived. The men had just come from their first meeting with the village's tribal elders, where they asked how the U.S. military could help the village residents. The women's translator was shocked to hear that they spoke fluent Arabic. The next morning, the soldiers would manage the first food distribution in weeks. UN rations had disappeared when the war had erupted nearly a month before. Pockets of the military were transforming overnight from aggressors to humanitarian relief workers, even if it was just aimed at winning Iraqi hearts and minds. Aid agencies had been critical of the military's fledgling relief work in Afghanistan, claiming that it endangered their own mission by blurring the line between the United States and the neutral humanitarian community, and now it was happening in Iraq. It was an historic moment. Marla didn't give a damn. All she cared about was getting to Baghdad as quickly as possible.

As the women sat under the stars, local villagers brought them chicken and rice, which they ate next to a roaring fire. They retired to their car for a few hours' sleep before the C-130 Hercules' scheduled arrival. The Special Forces soldiers promised to wake them up for the predawn spectacle. Scrambling out of the car when the men knocked on their window, they strapped on night goggles and clambered to the roof of a house.

The sky began to rumble, and like a giant prehistoric bird, the plane sailed over the village, releasing food rations and other supplies a short distance away. The packages, which even included a can of paint to blot out the village's one mural of Saddam Hussein, fluttered through the sky and thumped onto the desert floor. Its lights switched off, the plane vanished into the black sky as quickly as it had appeared. As the sun came up, the women ate breakfast with the Special Forces, excited by the experience. Still in the car, Marla slept through the whole thing.

Rousing from slumber, Marla was upset to find out that they wouldn't be leaving for another few hours. The other journalists wanted to stick around for the food distribution. A truck was dispatched to the drop site to collect the food. They snapped photographs and took notes as the Special Forces, working with the village elders, arranged the four hundred fifty residents into orderly lines in an old warehouse. They calmly explained what was about to occur. As the soldiers carefully monitored, volunteers passed out the first bundles of food in a post-Saddam Iraq. It was a once-in-a-lifetime experience, but it had no bearing on the fate of Iraqis who had been harmed by the bombing. For Marla, it was a distraction from what mattered most.

After collecting enough information for their stories and fueling up the car, the women started on the final leg of their journey, this time heading north. As soon as they hit the outskirts of Karbala, all hell broke loose. They weaved between frantic looters carting off stolen goods and dodged gun-waving men. The women were terrified. They pushed on and reached the ancient city of Babylon, only to be stopped at an American checkpoint. The soldiers had strict orders to let only military personnel and aid workers through to Baghdad, which was just thirty minutes away. The journalists turned on their satellite phones, desperately calling colleagues in Baghdad, hoping they could convince their military contacts to let them pass. Nothing worked. So they were sent on another five-hour detour through the Sunni Triangle, Iraq's most explosive region. Gunfire cracked all around them. Everyone in the car was frantic. They made feverish phone calls. Marla was completely zoned out, unable to do anything to help because she didn't have a phone. She nodded off, depressed, as bullets zipped past.

They finally made it to Baghdad in one piece, careening through the chaos of looters, tanks, and the *rat-a-tat* of automatic weapons. The second they rolled up to the Sheraton Hotel downtown, Marla sprang to life as if a switch had been flipped. She cheerily thanked the women for the ride, grabbed her things, and dashed off.

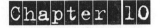

Operation Iraqi Compassion

(How to Treat an Injured Child)

Yes, a number is important, but it's not as important as making sure that we recognize each number as a human life.
—MARLA ON *Nightline* FROM BAGHDAD, SPRING 2003

Marla hit the ground running and didn't stop.
While many large organizations were spending thousands—
if not millions—of dollars to figure out how to get humanitarian projects providing food and medical relief up and running, the girl from California had already gotten down to business within days after the fall of Baghdad.

In the weeks and months that followed, she helped civilians wherever she could. When she wasn't collecting data on the dead and injured, she kept busy making friends with military personnel who had the ability to help civilians or finding proper medical care for wounded children. When she didn't possess the tools to accomplish a particular task, she alerted better-equipped experts who could. Iraq was expensive and explosive. She had no money and no security. At night, she dazzled exhausted journalists and other foreign friends by organizing her famous dancing parties.

Leaving her road trip companions behind at the Sheraton, Marla sprinted next door to the Palestine Hotel on Abu Nawas Street. Located on the east bank of the Tigris, it was one of the only hotels the Baath Party had sanctioned for members of the foreign press corps during the aerial raids, and also transplanted its own Information Ministry staff onto the premises. Directly across the river, Saddam's palace complex and government buildings lit up the night sky as they burned. The Information Ministry fled when Baghdad fell, but the Palestine remained the nerve center for the media.

Marla tore into the crowded hotel lobby, weaving through journalists, soldiers, and other foreigners to get to reception. The Iraqi concierge alerted the British *Sunday Times* suite. Jon rushed down and there was Marla, beaming, as if she'd appeared by magic. He was amazed she had managed to scramble to Baghdad so quickly after the fall. Jon was sharing his suite with two *Sunday Times* colleagues, a writer and a photographer. Quarters were cramped, but he agreed to allow Marla to stay with them for a day or two until other arrangements could be made.

As always, Jon was dedicating much of his coverage to the human impact of the war. No one had been more affected by the U.S. sweep than the residents in and around Hillah. Located roughly sixty miles south of Baghdad, the sleepy town is lined with date palms and surrounded by fields and farming villages. The Hillah tragedy began on March 31, when the U.S. Army began pushing north to Baghdad through the Karbala gap. They didn't want the Iraqis to know which route they were taking, so they devised a plan to confuse them. While the main thrust would continue up through Karbala, the army sent a number of decoy troops, known as a "feint," toward Hillah farther east. As the U.S. troops rolled into the south of town, they drew heavy fire from Saddam's Republican Guard. Much of it came from residential areas. The Iraqis had parked their tanks between homes and launched their rockets from backyards. They were heavily embedded in the civilian population, rendering ordinary people vulnerable to returning U.S. firepower.

In Hillah the American army's weapon of choice, which has been ardently criticized by groups like Human Rights Watch, was the Multiple Launch Rocket System. The army's longest-range ground weapon, each rocket contains nearly six hundred fifty cluster bombs, which are roughly the size and shape of a soda can. The army launches six rockets at a time—nearly four thousand cluster bombs for every shot. Upward of 20 percent of the bombs fail to explode upon impact. The fuse—a tiny white ribbon—often gets caught in tree branches. A child yanking at the innocuous-looking object will lose an arm at best. Whether the bombs maimed on impact or in the days to follow, the scale of civilian carnage that took place in Hillah was unparalleled in Iraq during those first few weeks of the U.S. invasion. More than five hundred people were wounded, their bodies sliced by shrapnel and their limbs blown off by cluster bombs. At least nineteen people were killed. While the coalition forces were working to topple the regime, the Iraqi Information Ministry used the horror of Hillah as propaganda—it was proof that the Americans were killing innocent civilians. They even shuttled the foreign press corps to the town's hospital on tour buses so they could glimpse the gore. Now that the regime was gone, Jon and his colleagues wanted to follow up on the story. Marla came along to investigate and begin to document the civilian tragedy of the war.

They drove down Hillah's main road, turning off at the hospital. Following the journalists' lead, Marla charged through the front entrance and came upon Dr. Falluji, a British-educated physician who was overwhelmed by the bloodshed. The halls were congested with grieving relatives and the wards filled with patients; many were children whose stumps were wrapped in bloody bandages. Marla tearfully offered her deepest sympathies and apologized on behalf of her country.

Unlike other Iraqi hospitals, Hillah's records were computerized and helpful for her survey. She normally had to sift through mountains of hand-scrawled documents to find what she needed. Jon lent Dr. Falluji his Thuraya mobile satellite phone to call family living in England to let them know he had survived the invasion and that he was safe. In return, the doctor escorted them to a nearby farm that was still littered with unexploded cluster bombs.

Back on the road, they noticed a group of U.S. soldiers at a school. Thinking fast, Marla yelled for the driver to stop. She darted out of the car and strutted straight toward them.

"Hi! I'm Marla!" she said. She asked them where they were from and how they were coping with life in Iraq.

They looked at her, bewildered by the sight of a perky California girl in the middle of Iraq, and couldn't help but smile. The men were detonating unexploded cluster bombs that had landed in the schoolyard. She told them about the bombs she saw at the farm, telling them to explode those as well before they killed or wounded somebody. Charmed, they gave her some pens and candy. She turned her back to pluck a sunflower from what was left of the school garden when a bone-jolting blast shook the earth. She spun around to a mushrooming cloud of smoke, another bomb made safe.

She began scouring Hillah and other areas outside of Baghdad, noting cluster bomb locations, often delivering the information to the Marines who held daily meetings with the humanitarian community at the Palestine. Once she and Jon were stopped by a military unit headed by a tough-looking sergeant. She knew where the bombs were, she said, and did he want the information? Grateful for the tip, they dispatched defusers to the sites. Before long, the military had nicknamed Marla "Cluster Bomb Girl."

Back in Baghdad, Marla began canvassing the main hotels. Smiling broadly, she handed everyone she met a fresh business card, explaining her mission and that she was looking for assistants. Many people she ran into were old friends from Kabul who were familiar with her work with civilian casualties, including Jon Lee Anderson, the *New Yorker* reporter at the Prom party. Another was Sam Zia-Zarifi of Human Rights Watch, who was both amused to see Kabul's socialite in Baghdad and impressed by how professional she now seemed.

The improvised networking came through. A few days after arriving in Baghdad, she entered the lobby at the al-Fanar, a small hotel across the street from the Palestine, and left with her Iraq Victims Compassion Campaign staff in place.

Marla had temporarily moved into a borrowed room at the al-Fanar. It had no electricity and little water, but she had the space to herself while her friend was away. Its restaurant, luckily, was equipped with functioning light switches and an affable waitstaff, making it one of the more popular gathering places in town. While the Palestine and Sheraton Hotels were teeming with staff working for large news outlets, the cozier yet ramshackle al-Fanar attracted freelance journalists and other reporters who had arrived after Baghdad fell. Several Iraqis were also seeking refuge there. Friends and family of the hotel's owner, who fled their homes before the bombing, considered the al-Fanar a safe haven due to its proximity to the Palestine. Its most famous resident, however, was a caged monkey who lived in the lobby. Journalists dubbed the belligerent primate "Karl Rove."

Faiz Ali Salim was looking for a job. The former Iraqi Airways pilot was having coffee with Thorne Anderson, Marla's friend from Islamabad and Kabul, at the al-Fanar to discuss working as his assistant. An Iraqi-American friend had recommended Faiz to the photojournalist as he left for Baghdad. Faiz wanted a well-paid position, he told Thorne, but was concerned about security and ideally wanted to spend his time helping his countrymen in some way. Thorne advised Faiz to work with Marla. Her civilian casualty survey work was much safer than Thorne's job, which could take them into the line of fire. Thorne saw Marla buzz into the lobby and waved. She bounced over, brightly greeting her old friend. Offering Faiz what little money she could spare, Marla hired him on the spot. Luckily, she didn't have to worry about living expenses. She knew her journalist friends would come through. Her own limited resources, earned as a consultant with the Vietnam Veterans of America Foundation and donated by individuals sympathetic to her cause, including her parents, were needed to help the Iraqis. She had several thousand dollars, but in Iraq, that money went fast.

Next was Raed Jarrar. He walked into the al-Fanar lobby with nothing but a business card reading "Iraqi Victims Compassion Campaign" and a description of a boisterous young blonde. A friend who met Marla at a party before the fall of Baghdad had given him Marla's card, explaining her mission in Iraq, which had intrigued him. Raed went to the al-Fanar to find Marla, inquiring about her at the front desk. When he approached her, Marla smiled but brusquely told him she'd get to him in a minute, when she was finished talking to Faiz.

Raed is highly educated, born into a comfortable and relatively modern household. Pale-skinned with light brown hair and a goatee, he could easily pass for an average American college student. He became famous—or at least his name did—when one of his closest friends started a blog called "Dear Raed." Written in letter form to Raed, who was studying architecture in Amman, Salam Pax described the atmosphere in Baghdad in the months leading up to the war. The candid accounts drew international attention, and the mysterious

Salam soon became known as the "Baghdad Blogger." One month before the war began, Raed left the safety of Amman to be with his family and friends in Baghdad. Now that the first phase of the war was over, he wanted to apply his education to documenting the human cost of the U.S. invasion. When Marla finished up with Faiz, she sat down with Raed and hired him as her partner. He had the connections and the technical skills needed to turn her concept of starting an Iraqi civilian casualty survey into reality.

Borrowing friends' satellite phones and Internet connections, Marla stayed in constant touch with Tim Rieser and bounced ideas off him. As Baghdad was falling, he advised her to get a civilian casualty survey up and running immediately. He and Senator Leahy were pushing for legislation guaranteeing the same help for Iraqi victims as their Afghan counterparts. With assurances that an effective and U.S.-friendly professional—meaning Marla—was on the ground identifying civilian casualties, they would have more luck convincing Washington to support assistance. On April 16, 2003, less than a week after Marla arrived in Baghdad, they succeeded. Because of the legislation passed on that day, the government would later allocate an astonishing ten million dollars to assist Iraqi victims.

Guarantees of some form of assistance seemed to be evolving into accepted wartime policy by Washington. The only problem was that Washington didn't have an office, or even an individual, to manage the civilian casualty count and claims. Impoverished and unprotected, Marla was carrying a governmental and military burden on her own shoulders. As long as nobody else was taking charge, she thought, it was her responsibility.

On April 4, Zahra Kathem and her family were fleeing the firestorm in Baghdad when a bomb struck their taxi. As the car burst into flames, her mother threw three-year-old Zahra and her three-month-old sister, Hawra, out the open window. The baby miraculously escaped with no more than a few superficial nicks and burns. Her mother, father, and five other siblings burned to death moments after the strike. Two weeks later, Zahra was close to death. She had little hope of surviving.

In the wave of looting that swept across Baghdad, many hospitals had been gutted, and medical supplies were impossible to find. Dr. Bilal al-Radaeei inspected the second- and third-degree burns that had charred Zahra's face, back, arms, and legs.

"Cold, cold," Zahra wailed, trembling uncontrollably. "Cover me, Mommy. Where are you, Daddy? I'm cold."

Zahra's grandmother, the girl's closest surviving relative, sat at her bedside imploring, "Please help my little girl Zahra. Please do not let her die. Please make her better for me."

Earlier, Marla had been inspired by the military's swift response to another crisis. Journalists had stumbled upon a twelve-year-old boy named Ali at Baghdad's al-Kindi Hospital during the bombing raids. A couple of weeks before, a U.S. bomb had flattened Ali's home in southeastern Baghdad. One of his forearms had been burned off, and the other was a bloody pulp. His torso was scorched black. Ali's immediate family, eight relatives in all, had died in the attack. Doctors predicted he had only weeks to live before septicemia, a lethal infection that commonly strikes burn victims, consumed him. Aided by horrifying photographs of the injured boy, several foreign correspondents rallied U.S. forces to evacuate Ali to a facility that could better treat him. The military agreed, flying him to Ibn Sina Hospital's Center for Burns and Plastic Surgery in Kuwait City. He was saved and fitted with prosthetic arms. Ali effectively became a poster boy of sorts, showing that the United States cared about ordinary Iraqis it had harmed.

Daily, Marla attended every meeting between the Marines and the aid community at the Palestine, soaking up information and making connections. Ali was a hot topic of discussion during one meeting, and Marla approached the head of the Marines' health unit.

"I'm really happy to hear about Ali, that's such great work!" she told him brightly before sobering her tone. "But, you know, he's only one child. I'm going to the hospitals every day, and there are so many injured civilians. If I find more people who need to be evacuated so they can survive, will you help them, too?"

"Absolutely, just come here to the hotel and give us the information. We'll do whatever we can," he promised.

On April 18, Good Friday, Jon told Marla about Zahra. Unfortunately, the Marines she'd met at the Palestine, with whom she'd already established a good rapport, were being replaced by the army the next day. Jon said that Zahra might only have twenty-four hours to live.

The next day at the Palestine, soldiers, journalists, and aid workers swarmed about. Army units were now patrolling out front instead of the Marines. Cars that had managed to pass through the army's razor-wired checkpoints clogged the street. It was a mob. Marla pushed her way through the crowd to one of the soldiers.

"Hi, I'm Marla! I've got a serious situation and I need your help!" she screamed above the grinding roar of two large generators that coughed up clouds of exhaust. The soldier stared at Marla blankly. She didn't give him a moment to think.

"I work with Iraqis who were harmed in the bombing. I know the Marines, and they promised me they'd medevac injured people like that little boy Ali who they took to Kuwait. Well, there's a little girl in the burn hospital who was hit by a bomb and she's doing really bad. The doctors say she'll die really soon if she doesn't get better care!" Marla shouted over the generators.

"Sorry, I'd like to help, but I don't know what I can do."

"Okay, but who *can* help me? I mean, she's seriously going to *die!*" Marla pushed on.

"Well, the only thing I can suggest is that you go to the hospital and talk to the army unit guarding it. Maybe they can do something."

"Thank you *sooo* much, you rock!"

Now she just had to figure out how to get there. Bob Arnott, an MSNBC journalist and medical doctor, had expressed interest in covering Zahra's story. He was bound to have a driver. She bolted up to his room and told him it was time to go, but he wasn't ready. Growing frantic, she insisted that Zahra's life depended on leaving immediately, and he relented.

Rushing back downstairs, Bob led the way to his driver's taxi. After breaking free of a traffic jam, they began careening through the city's streets. The plundering of Baghdad had continued, and packs of men and boys looted anything they could find, from appliances to food. The passengers hunkered down at the sound of gunshots in the streets. After forty-five minutes, Marla's patience had worn out. She'd been told the hospital was a twenty-minute drive away. Marla asked the driver why it was taking so long, and he explained that he'd taken a detour to avoid even more explosive sections of town. A few minutes later, they finally rounded a corner and screeched to a halt in front of al-Karameh Hospital. A U.S. Army Bradley tank was parked out front, protecting the facility from looters.

She dashed out of the car, rushing toward the tank. Two young African-American soldiers gripped their weapons, looking tense and uneasy. Marla repeated her story to the stunned men, begging them to let her pass. They unlocked the gate and let her and Bob through.

When Marla first laid eyes on Zahra, she was horrified. The little girl was enclosed in what appeared to be a wooden cage. Dr. al-Radaeei leaned over her small body, careful not to touch her. He removed the crude, homemade structure that balanced over her head and torso on a rickety bed frame. The cage prevented the sheets from coming into direct contact with her raw, singed skin. Gently peeling back the blanket so Marla and Bob could see the girl's injuries, Dr. al-Radaeei sucked in his breath to keep steady. All Marla could distinguish were swaths of loose bandages clinging to charred flesh. Despite the doctor's controlled hand, the blanket lightly rubbed against Zahra's body. She opened what was barely recognizable as a mouth and let out a harrowing scream that echoed through the bare hospital ward. The ward's other patients, who had all been burned in work-related or domestic accidents, languished in similar cages, unmoving and listless.

If Zahra didn't die from the burns that covered 90 percent of her body, Dr. al-Radaeei explained, she would inevitably perish soon from a septicemia infection. Trying to stay composed, his sorrowful eyes betrayed an overwhelming sense of helplessness. Like many professionals in Iraq who study abroad, he had been trained in England and was used to having the supplies he needed to treat his patients. Although American soldiers guarding the front entrance meant that al-Karameh Hospital was spared the rampant looting, the war prevented the doctor from restocking basic yet vital supplies like oxygen, drugs, and clean water.

"We could help her ourselves, but the war, the war," Dr. al-Radaeei said, his voice trailing off as he replaced the cage.

There was no more time to waste. Leaving Bob behind, Marla ran out the front exit and toward the hulking tank.

"Hi, I'm Marla! Look, we have to get a helicopter here immediately to save that girl's life in there!"

"I'm not sure I can do that, ma'am," one of the soldiers said.

"That girl inside was severely burned when her family's car was hit by an American bomb. We've examined her, and I can verify that it's true. If she doesn't get better care *now*, she's not going to make it, and we can help her!"

The private signaled to his partner, realizing how serious she was, but there wasn't much they could do without their superiors' clearance. At the very least, they had to confirm Marla's story themselves, so they started inside. Marla jogged after the soldiers, keeping pace with their long strides.

Marla introduced the soldiers to Dr. al-Radaeei, who led the way to the burn unit. The soldiers slowly took in the scene before them and began inspecting Zahra and the other patients, meticulously recording their names and other personal information into a small notebook.

"We don't have any more time to lose, let's get her out of here!" Marla finally blurted.

After they collected the information, one of the soldiers told the doctor they would do their best to help Zahra, then turned to leave. Marla scurried after them.

"I'm coming up there too!" she hollered at the soldiers as they scaled the tank.

The soldier who seemed to be in charge of the situation turned. Offering his hand, he hauled Marla up and onto the tank, her blue dress fluttering behind her. Gunshots rang out somewhere nearby, but she didn't flinch.

"Listen, we are wasting time here and we are playing with that little girl's life. Don't you want to save her? You can do it! Help me get her out of here!" she instructed him, her hands placed firmly on her hips.

The soldier pondered for a moment and then turned to say something to his partner that she couldn't hear. He then spoke into the radio mouthpiece embedded into his helmet, removed it from his head, and placed it onto

Marla's. She looked up at him, but the helmet fell down over her eyes. Readjusting it, she asked him what she had to do.

"Go ahead, Miss Marla. Go ahead. Tell him what you told me."

A voice crackled over the helmet's radio. It was the soldier's commanding officer.

"Hi, this is Marla! There's a three-year-old girl here at Karameh Hospital who was hit by an American bomb and she's badly burned. She's going to die unless we evacuate her to a better hospital. Over," she said, waiting for a response.

"Okay, do you have the hospital paperwork detailing the cause of her injuries? Over," the voice replied.

"Yeah, we've got it all here, and I've looked at the girl myself along with a doctor. Over."

"Good copy. Hold tight, Marla. We'll be there soon. Over."

The soldier plucked the helmet from her head and spoke tersely into his mouthpiece once again. Scampering down the side of the tank, Marla rushed back into the hospital to deliver the good news to Dr. al-Radaaei.

When she told him about Zahra's impending evacuation, he asked, "But what about the others, Miss Marla? I can only do so much to treat them here."

She didn't think the army would agree to evacuate the patients who weren't injured by U.S. firepower. The doctor was happy for Zahra, but distraught for the other patients. A couple of nurses draped the other patients' cages with blankets, so they wouldn't witness Zahra's evacuation, and they began preparing the girl for her departure.

Within minutes, the distant thump of a U.S. Army medevac helicopter turned into an ear-splitting howl. A bank robbery was under way close by, and the helicopter disappeared to find a safer place to touch down. Several minutes later, an armored Humvee thundered down the street and stopped next to the tank. Four army medics jumped out. With Marla in tow, the soldiers ran over. Marla begged them to evacuate the other burn victims as well as Zahra. After quick deliberation, they decided they had room for three patients. Dr. al-Radaaei made the painful decision, then Bob, the army medics, the doctor, and the nurses all lifted Zahra and the other two patients into an ambulance.

"Allahu Akbar! Allahu Akbar!" God is great, God is great, a relative of one of the patients cried as the Humvee disappeared down the street toward the helicopter, the ambulance wailing behind. Bob jumped into his taxi and trailed after them to film the spectacle.

Marla collapsed against the hospital wall, her hands shaking. It occurred to her that she'd forgotten to ask where the army was taking Zahra. She walked over to the soldier who'd helped evacuate her. He didn't know where the patients were going, he said, but was sure that they would be well cared for.

"You have to go and tell your mother what you've done," Marla said to the soldier.

"I thought of my own two daughters back home. I was just doin' my job, ma'am," he responded in a southern drawl.

The following evening, Marla and Jon went to Nabil restaurant, a favorite journalist haunt in Baghdad's Mansour district, to celebrate. They were joined at the newly opened eatery by several friends, including Hala Jabar, the *Sunday Times* reporter who first found Zahra. Halfway through the meal, Marla realized it was Easter Sunday. She grabbed Jon's Thuraya satellite telephone and ran outside. Pointing the antenna toward the sky to establish a signal, Marla called home.

"Hi Mom! Happy Easter!"

Marla heard muffled sobs at the other end of the delayed line. Nancy was crying with relief. She hadn't heard from her daughter since Marla had left Amman nearly two weeks before.

Chapter 11

American Beauty

(How to Look Good on Camera)

The Pentagon says they have no policy and they're not going to put any effort in doing a formal count of how many civilians were killed or look at these cases. That's wrong. How do we prevent these cases from happening in the future if we don't investigate every incident where a civilian is harmed?

—MARLA IN A RADIO RECORDING
WITH QUIL LAWRENCE, BAGHDAD, MAY 2003

All the Club Kabul members were delighted to see Marla—and she them. Like David Wright of ABC News and Sam of Human Rights Watch, everyone noticed the shift in her from radical activist to human rights professional. She also appeared disproportionately undaunted by the violence and chaos of Iraq. When Marla faced struggles of her own in Iraq, she pushed through them, masking any anxieties behind hard work and her booming laugh. She focused on helping others, rooting for all her friends, when she probably needed a cheerleader of her own. As time went on, Marla often slipped notes of encouragement under her friends' hotel doors. While Marla had the occasional pick-me-up by e-mail or long-distance phone call, she rarely had someone to console her after a long day risking her life to help others.

Jon moved to the Al-Hamra Hotel, which is commonly known to journalists as simply "the Hamra," in Baghdad's Jadiriyah district. The Hamra was tucked away on a small side street, making it better protected from rocket-propelled grenade attacks than the other hotels. It was fast becoming Baghdad's journalist hub. Many news outlets rented out spacious—if dated and dilapidated—suites where they worked, slept, and threw parties. Jon let Marla use one of the large rooms in the *Sunday Times* suite as her office. As in Kabul, Marla was one of the only nonjournalists that the media, wary of many relief and human rights workers, let into their exclusive club.

Marla liked the Hamra and felt at home there. It had a dreary restaurant claiming to be Chinese—the perfect venue for her future salsa parties. Most important, it had a sparkling outdoor pool, sandwiched between the Hamra's two towers. She wouldn't have to go far for her marathon morning and evening swims.

It was by the pool where Marla ran into Catherine (Cat) Philp, an attractive *Times* of London reporter. They'd first met at a party in Kabul in the spring of 2002, when Marla dragged Cat out onto the dance floor to salsa.

Cat, a self-possessed Scot with long, light auburn hair, was trying to get comfortable in a lounge chair by the pool. Marla was gliding through the water like a seal as Cat grimaced in pain. Finishing her workout, Marla popped out of the pool and spotted her friend with her arm in a sling. Marla was immediately concerned and rushed to her side, still dripping with water. As it turned out, Cat had survived a car crash journeying from northern Iraq to Baghdad, dislocating several ribs, but she was determined to stay on and cover the aftermath of the fall of Baghdad.

"Oh my God, sweetie! Oh my God, are you okaaaay? What happened?"

Within minutes Marla was fussing over Cat, asking her how she could help, if she could get her anything, even though she hardly knew her at the time. Not knowing what else to do and wanting to please, Marla treated Cat to one of her famous massages, putting a smile on the composed woman's face.

Cat noticed that Marla seemed to be doing well and appeared glad to be back where it was all happening, sinking her teeth into her human rights work. She also observed that her curvier salsa figure from Kabul had disappeared. The girl before her was rail thin, if toned. There was a "whisper" floating around the Hamra about Marla's weight loss: "Oh my God, have you seen Marla?"

CIVIC was accomplishing tasks with a miniscule fraction of the resources that other NGOs and aid agencies had. Even the smaller outfits have at least a handful of seasoned employees: a fund-raiser, an accountant, an operations manager, an administrator, a media-relations officer, a web designer. Although she had indispensable assistance from Faiz and Raed in the day-to-day functions of the Iraq surveys, the twenty-six-year-old "bubblehead" from California was filling several full-time positions herself. Not only that, she was already making great strides in the war-ravaged country before other NGOs even arrived.

Faiz always accompanied Marla when she traveled. He was her translator, driver, and man of all trades. They went to Saddam's old palace complex, now known as the Green Zone, for meetings with the army and American and Iraqi government officials. They went to Baghdad hospitals and civilian homes, collecting casualty data. Faiz, who was much more fastidious than Marla, kept her files and schedule in order. Although Faiz spent more time on the road than Marla, she joined him on many trips outside of Baghdad. They retraced the U.S. military's advance on Baghdad in reverse. The sweep left its scar on cities lining the route from the Kuwait border to Baghdad—as well as some northern Iraqi towns. There were thousands of suspected civilian casualties, and Marla and Faiz braved the incredibly dangerous roads together to carry out their mission. Iraqis weren't as welcoming to the Americans as the Afghans had been, and they were entering neighborhoods and cities where many residents despised anything representing a U.S. occupation, and Marla was about as American as it got.

Although Marla had the idea, it was Raed who managed the surveys. The young Iraqi graduate student used his family contacts to recruit one hundred fifty volunteers, all of them medical professionals, throughout Iraq. The teams divided the country, scouring the south—Basra, Najaf, Karbala, and Nasiriyah, the worst hit. To the west, they covered Fallujah and Ramadi. Raed even traveled to the northern towns of Mosul and Kirkuk to supervise data collection there. They had little money—only what Marla's private donors had given her.

Marla spent most of her time on the road with Faiz. But she often joined Raed on expeditions in Baghdad too, and sometimes outside of the city limits. Raed had seen Marla wave down Baghdad "taxicabs," often no more than a private vehicle whose owner was in need of a buck, as if she were in the East Village. Usually dressed in a figure-hugging outfit or a sundress, her blond hair whipping in the desert wind, Marla jumped in at will—sometimes at night and sometimes inebriated. Once inside, she boldly haggled with the driver over a dollar or two. When they went to Najaf, a holy Shiite town in the south, so Raed could look into surveys, Raed was prepared for the worst.

"Marla, I'm just not comfortable with you coming. It could be really dangerous for you there," Raed said.

"Don't worry! Everything will be fine. I'll put on an *abaya* so I don't stand out so much," she said, referring to the traditional black robe and veil.

Raed relented with a sigh, and they jumped into a taxi for the journey south to Najaf. They pulled up near the town's main shrine, a large, brown, fortressed structure topped with a golden dome. Before Raed got out, he carefully instructed Marla to stay put.

"I promise, I'll stay here! Don't worry, just go do your work and I'll see you when you get back," she assured him.

Not trusting her, Raed told the driver in Arabic to make sure Marla didn't leave the car, and then headed off. A few minutes later, making sure the coast was clear, she opened the door and tiptoed out. Ignoring the driver's protestations, she hopped toward the shrine's blue-tiled entryway. When he returned a short while later, Raed panicked when he didn't see Marla in the car.

"How could you let her go? She doesn't even speak Arabic!" he yelled at the driver.

Raed dashed into the street, scanning the crowds for Marla. He was sure that her hair was uncovered—something that would anger the locals. Some bystanders noticed Raed frantically running through the streets and called out to him. He was wearing Western clothes, so they addressed him in English.

"Mister, mister, come here!" they called in English, assuming he was with the mysterious blonde. He followed them to the front of the shrine, and there she was, surrounded by about fifty Iraqis.

She was wearing her *abaya* halfway, the Marla way. Raed thought someone was going to kill them. But then he noticed that everyone seemed to be smiling, if a bit confused. Marla was shaking hands with men, women, and children.

"I'm sorry, I'm sorry. I'm, like, *so* sorry we invaded your country! I'm *so* sorry we killed your people!" she apologized in English to each person as she shook his or her hand. They couldn't understand a word she was saying, but they did understand that she was kind.

Marc Garlasco had been with Human Rights Watch for just a week as their military analyst. His previous job was at the Pentagon, where he'd worked for seven years. His final task at the Department of Defense was recommending Iraqi bombing targets to the U.S. military. If there were too many lives at stake for any particular target, for example, Marc would put forth a dissenting opinion to his superiors. As in Afghanistan, the United States prioritized minimizing civilian death and harm—but it was impossible to avoid completely.

Now it was late April, and he was in the country to apply his expertise to a Human Rights Watch report evaluating the military's performance—with a civilian casualty angle—in its air and ground wars.

Marc had met Marla briefly on his first night in Iraq through his colleagues. He later ran into Marla in Baghdad.

"Hi, sweetie, how are you?" she greeted him before quickly changing gears. "Okay, so, here's what you need to do. You have to go to Hillah for your report. There was a huge cluster strike there and there were lots of civilian casualties. There's this doctor there in the hospital called Dr. Falluji and he's the dude to talk to. Tell him I sent you."

He eventually took Marla's advice, making the trip down to Hillah with his team.

Dr. Falluji glared at the Human Rights Watch researchers. Turning his nose up, he refused to accommodate them.

"I don't have time to help you. You see how many patients I have," he snapped.

"I'm sorry you don't have time for us, Dr. Falluji, but Marla said you'd take care of us," Marc shot back, giving it another try.

The doctor's face brightened.

"You know Miss Marla?" he said, remembering the girl who was helping the military clear cluster bombs from the area and helping civilian victims get assistance.

"Oh, yes. She gave me your name and said you'd help us

out," Marc pressed on, noticing he'd piqued the doctor's interest.

"Come, come. Follow me!"

For the next three days, Dr. Falluji took them around Hillah and all the villages. He gave them copies of all the hospital records of civilian casualties, both deaths and injuries. He even invited them for tea in his house one day. Simply dropping the name "Marla" in Iraq opened doors.

A few weeks had passed since Zahra's evacuation, and Marla still had no idea where the little girl had been taken. She was growing anxious and concerned. Faiz had been in fairly regular contact with Zahra's grandmother and other relatives, and they were desperate to know how the three-year-old was faring. Marla made numerous inquiries and had even submitted a formal request to the army on behalf of the family, asking after her condition and whereabouts. They had put all their hope into Zahra's survival, having lost so much already.

One May afternoon, Marla approached Major Watkins with the army's 3rd Infantry Division.

"Have you heard anything about Zahra yet?" she asked.

The major looked Marla in the eye, hesitating for a moment before delivering the news.

"I just received word. I'm so sorry, Marla. She didn't make it, but she was a real fighter," he said, informing her that Zahra had spent the past weeks in a military hospital camp in the desert. "She survived the external burns, but she couldn't fight off the septicemia infection. I'm very sorry."

Marla began crying hysterically on Major Watkins' shoulder. A Human Rights Watch researcher soon took over holding Marla. The major stood by, watching, unable to do anything. Marla finally disentangled herself and ran out into the dry evening air. Humvees and slick new SUVs kicked up dust as they passed her. Her head was throbbing.

Marla walked aimlessly through the Green Zone, fishing for a borrowed Thuraya satellite phone in her massive bag. The wide boulevard was strewn with shell casings and other detritus left over from the army's recent assault. She called Jon, who had returned to London. She began crying into the phone when she heard his voice.

The following day Marla and Faiz climbed into Faiz's car and started toward a working-class neighborhood on Baghdad's outskirts. It was the most difficult duty of her life.

Marla knocked on the front gate. It opened and a man in his forties, Zahra's uncle, looked down at her expectantly. After announcing who had arrived, the girl's grandmother appeared. The old woman was dressed in an *abaya* and wore a hopeful expression on her face. She was holding Zahra's four-month-old sister, who had survived the attack.

"Is my baby Zahra walking yet? When is she coming home?" she asked.

Faiz spoke in Arabic and the old woman began to wail. She needed somewhere to place her outrage. And at that moment, Marla was her only target, the blond image of America itself, delivering such painful news.

"Saddam hurt us and now you Americans are hurting us!" she howled.

"I'm so sorry, I'm so sorry that Zahra died. I wish I could have done more. I'm so sorry. I promise you, I promise I will get you some help for your loss. I promise I won't leave you. I won't forget you or Zahra," Marla wept.

If only I had saved her everything would be okay, Marla thought. But everything was not okay. Marla soon began having nightmares. In them, Zahra's disfigured face and that of her agonized grandmother implored, "Why, why, why couldn't you save us?"

More than a year later, unable to shake the memory himself, Major Watkins wrote to Marla that her compassion had been a bright spot amid so much tragedy.

Marla's journalist friends were increasingly interested in covering her work helping civilians. She brought several camera crews to Hillah to report on its tragedy. Her friend Quil Lawrence, who worked for Public Radio International's "The World" program, coproduced by the BBC, began recording her. Overcome by Zahra's death and the pain she was witnessing, a bit of Marla's old intensity came out. Her rhetoric, however, was much more tempered and focused than it had been in the past. She repeatedly came back to a critical point that she couldn't let go: The United States must conduct civilian casualty surveys of its own. In one recording session, she speaks rapidly and emotionally:

"Whereas the U.S. government said from the very beginning of the campaign that they would go to great lengths to minimize civilian casualties, and we do believe they did that, the next thing they have to do is they have to do their own investigation to look at where civilians were harmed. You can't just simply say as a policy that you're going to protect and do everything you can to minimize what they call collateral damage, a word I *hate*, because when you go out door-to-door you meet the families. It's not just a number and collateral damage is a husband, a wife, a child. They're people, they're families and they deserve all of their cases to be investigated. So if the U.S. does have this policy they need to do their own survey and they need to offer economic help and assistance to help people who were harmed in this campaign to rebuild their lives.

"It doesn't matter if you were for or against the war or how great the political outcome is, innocent civilians should not be harmed in conflict and when they are, you must investigate the case and you must help them reconstruct their lives. And as the U.S. administration said from the very beginning, if one Iraqi's life is made worse because of a result of this campaign, then we have failed. So our goal is to help the U.S. meet their promise and to help Iraq get back on with its reconstruction and reconciliation process and the first thing is to help the innocent civilians who were harmed in this conflict. We saw what Saddam Hussein did to hundreds of thousands of people. Now let's help the U.S. get Iraq on its right feet by assisting those who got hurt."

Marla worked out of a clinic of sorts run by an Iraqi civilian assistance organization in Baghdad's Shiite slum, recently renamed Sadr City. It was an incredibly dangerous neighborhood. In a cluttered, dusty room, she recorded data of Iraqis who had been injured or lost homes and loved ones. Word had spread on the street that the young American was collecting information about their losses in order to find them some assistance, and people filed into the cramped room in force. When Marla told David Wright of ABC News about her recent work, he immediately pitched the story to the network's magazine program, *Nightline*. It was an easy sell.

In the *Nightline* video, Marla patiently waits as a soldier runs a metal detector around her body at the Green Zone entrance. She now had only fifty dollars left to her name, David reports. During sit-down interviews, she speaks coolly and calmly in ordinary but powerful terms about the work her organization, which she had just renamed Civilian Campaign for Innocent Victims in Conflict, is conducting in Baghdad and other cities. Her hair is neatly pulled back. She is incredibly diplomatic, choosing her words carefully. Marla had become the eloquent face and voice of CIVIC—and in many ways, a new face of America in Iraq.

Although she was both financially and emotionally strapped, the *Nightline* segment gave Marla the boost she desperately needed to continue on.

Chapter 12

Ten-Million-Dollar Baby

(How to Be a Fund-Raiser
Without an Office)

Recent terrorist attacks have created a rapidly deteriorating security situation, forcing many aid groups to leave Iraq. Consequently, CIVIC's role has greatly expanded. CIVIC needs the public to know about civilians killed or harmed in the conflict in order to bring more assistance to those in need. Please have your friends sign up on the list serve so they can read updates about the situation in Iraq. CIVIC will also be launching a campaign for the holiday season that will allow people to make donations.
—MARLA IN HER ONLINE JOURNAL ON
CIVIC'S WEBSITE, NOVEMBER 2003

After two months charging around war-torn Iraq, Marla left in early June for a short break. She had wanted to visit Jon in late May, but, he told her, he would be visiting his young son in South Africa at that time. So instead, Marla went back to Washington.

Along with Raed and Faiz, she had worked tirelessly gathering information for the surveys, witnessing human suffering on a daily—and sometimes hourly—basis. The mission was nowhere near completed, and she was beginning to fray emotionally and psychologically. She ached for money, and she had to stay on top of the U.S. government–allocated Iraqi War Victims Fund. Passing the law was a triumph; but the families still needed to receive the assistance. Many friends noticed she was drinking too much. She was celebrating, but also trying to drown her emotional demons, which were only enhanced by the psychological stress caused by her work and peripatetic lifestyle.

At around this time, Marla also tapped into her wider community to earn CIVIC some fast cash. Through her well-connected friends in Washington, she met wealthy businessmen sympathetic to her cause—and unsympathetic to the American occupation—at parties and more intimate gatherings. She talked about her work with passion and, on lucky nights, went home with promises for donations. In late May one individual threw her a lifeline, pledging to donate several thousand dollars.

The only thing she didn't quite get around to doing was trudging through the tedious paperwork required to set CIVIC up as a legitimate NGO. She'd looked into it but didn't follow through.

Marla had first met David Frankel and his friend Tom Ballanco back in 2000 at the national Green Party Convention in Denver. David, an intellectual property and business lawyer who represents companies doing "conscious work," wore earrings, dark blond dreadlocks, and a scraggly goatee. Marla gave David her card at the end of the dinner, and she logged him onto her long list of Green Party friends.

Marla got in touch with David after she had just returned to Baghdad, where she and Raed and Faiz were finishing up the civilian casualty survey. She then planned to return to the United States for a monthlong visit. Over e-mail, David offered to help get CIVIC off the ground legally and to hook Marla up with a friend and potential donor in San Francisco.

When she was back in California in early August, Marla took him up on his offer. They drove north across the Golden Gate Bridge, swathed in fog, and entered Marin. Cutting through the undulating bluffs straddling Highway 101, they soon exited at Larkspur, a tranquil community of million-dollar homes nestled among the redwoods. They drove down Magnolia Avenue to Roxanne's, an organic restaurant serving green concoctions in martini glasses and "raw" dishes for the price of a Maine lobster tail.

The donor was already waiting for them when they arrived. A few days before, David had called him up to pitch Marla, CIVIC, and its financial needs. Intrigued, he agreed to meet the young do-gooder. They sat down and Marla expertly delved into the genesis of her work, stopping inter-mittently to toss out a compliment or crack an outrageous or self-deprecating joke that left her and the others guffawing.

When they finished up with their food, the music-business millionaire and aging Deadhead dutifully pulled out his checkbook and reached for a pen. He handed the check to Marla without hesitation. She looked down and couldn't believe her eyes. He had just given her ten thousand dollars.

❖ ❖ ❖

After a quick stopover in Washington, Marla boarded a plane to Amman. By the time she arrived the next day, August 19, 2003, the UN Headquarters at the Canal Hotel in Baghdad had been bombed in a terrorist attack. The blast killed twenty-two people, many of them foreign humanitarian experts, including Sergio Vieira de Mello, UN Secretary-General Kofi Annan's special envoy in Iraq. More than a hundred others were injured.

Marla was shaken. The senseless attack marked a deadly turning point in Iraq. Insurgent groups, including al-Qaeda, led in Iraq by Jordanian-born Abu Musab al-Zarqawi, had gained in strength. Most UN staff were evacuated out of the country.

Marla stayed on. She and Raed were putting the final touches on the surveys. But they hit some rocky terrain. USAID, which had been helping to pay for CIVIC's employees and volunteer expenses in Iraq, withdrew its support. Like the time she was fired from her first job at the Rainforest Action Network in San Francisco, there is a bit of confusion as to why. Marla once implied that the head of USAID, Andrew Natsios, saw Marla's work as too politically controversial, so he pulled the plug. She claimed that they had initially promised her $100,000 to finish up her work, but the money never came. Marla also suggested to friends that Raed may have tried to court USAID money away from her—and toward his own NGO aspirations. Raed's story differs. He indicated that orders came "from above" for USAID to cut ties with American citizens, leading to the end of its funding relationship with CIVIC.

Over the next couple of months Raed and Marla continually butted heads. Both very strong-willed, they had different visions for their survey. Marla, Raed, Faiz, and their team of one hundred fifty surveyors documented that between the beginning of the war, on March 20, and May 1, U.S. military operations had resulted in 1,758 civilian deaths; 3,765 injuries; and 1,657 seriously damaged or destroyed homes and other civic structures. They had collected all the names and details of the tragedies, along with personal stories and photographs. These were only a portion of the casualties; there were some areas too dangerous to reach, and the casualties they counted occurred during a narrow window of time. President Bush declared the end of major combat operations on May 1. But the war, obviously, continued, shifting to a fight against the insurgency, which resulted in more civilian casualties. Nonetheless, their survey was massive. Raed wanted to make a big splash. Marla refused.

Marla was now steadily "navigating really ambiguous terrain," as her former Global Exchange friend Michael Shellenberger put it. Some thought it was dangerous ground as well. Raed was concerned that Marla was getting too friendly with the occupation government. She was working closely with them—along with the military—but only to ensure that the victims received U.S. assistance.

Marla did not want to risk upsetting her new valuable allies. Raed, however, was afraid the military would use the survey for its own propaganda machine and preferred to publish the report as soon as possible for maximum impact. Marla didn't share this view—and the survey had been her baby anyway, even if he had provided invaluable assistance. She had hired Raed to help *her*, she thought, not the reverse. He wasn't going to tell her what to do.

"Why did we put all these hundreds of people working the last four months?" Raed spat at her.

"We don't want to publish it just yet. We have to wait!" Marla sputtered back.

That was the end of their working relationship. CIVIC Iraq had been downsized to two: Marla and Faiz.

Charles Heatley was about to arrive for dinner. As the Coalition Provisional Authority's chief spokesman in Baghdad, he was a hard-won guest, and the evening's host, Adam Davidson, was fussing. The National Public Radio reporter wanted everything to be perfect. Other guests that early November evening would include several journalists who also lived in the house. They were Jen Banbury, Adam's girlfriend, who wrote for *Salon*; Christina Asquith, a *Christian Science Monitor* freelancer; and her boyfriend, Jack Fairweather, a correspondent with the UK's *Telegraph* newspaper. Two Canadians, video journalist Tara Sutton and Patrick Graham, who covered the war for *Harper's* magazine and other publications, were joining as well. There was a bit of snobbery attached to Adam's house; its tenants and short-term guests sought a more authentic Iraqi experience than other journalists who stuck to the more Westernized bubble of the Hamra Hotel.

The ambitious young reporters were all anxious to dine—and drink—with Heatley. The idea was to get the Briton, described as a swaggering James Bond character, warmed up with several glasses of wine so as to loosen his tongue. The Green Zone smokescreen was frustrating the journalists. Anything Heatley revealed during the evening would remain strictly off the record but would provide them with deeper insight on the strange workings of the occupation's mind.

The security situation in Iraq was spiraling daily, with the emergence of Jaish Ansar al-Sunna, or Army of the Protectors of the Sunna, an umbrella organization of Islamic guerrillas fighting the U.S. occupation. Terrorist attacks in Baghdad and other explosive cities like Fallujah were now a daily, if not hourly, occurrence. Hundreds of civilians were dying in the blasts. Margaret Hassan, the director of Care International in Iraq, had been executed by her captors a few days before. In October a car bomb exploded outside the Baghdad offices of the International Committee of the Red Cross. The most intrepid of aid agencies, they pulled their international staff out of the country. Marla was one of the only foreign humanitarian workers who stuck around, and she didn't have any security. Baghdad was becoming so violent that Adam and his tenants grew accustomed to the sounds of the insurgency:

"Most nights we would hear gunfire, maybe an explosion or two. We learned to differentiate. Car bombs made the floors shake; rocket-propelled grenades popped; mortars made a distinctive whoosh."

Like Marla, the journalists began drinking more heavily than they normally would to cope with the stress.

Jen and Christina were busy preparing the meal in the kitchen: fresh okra, coleslaw, a tomato and cucumber salad, and Christina's specialty, a chicken banana dish. They'd bought the ingredients at a grocery store and vegetable market near their house in Baghdad's upscale Jadiriyah district. They placed several bowls of food on the table, along with four or five bottles of wine. Soon after, the guest of honor, dressed in a leather bomber jacket, hopped off his motorcycle and strutted into the house with a helmet tucked under his arm.

After exchanging pleasantries, they all turned to sit down at the long dining table when Tara and Patrick made an entrance—with a wobbly Marla in tow. She clomped over to the group in her knee-high black boots with square, hollow heels. Marla loved her red wine, and clearly she'd already had some. She shot everyone a huge smile. Never sparkling white, her teeth were stained a purple-grayish hue. She began to prattle. After gushing over Jen and Adam for a minute, Marla noticed someone she hadn't met yet.

"Hi! I'm Marla! And who are *you*?" she burbled to Christina, who is also blond, cute, and vivacious, yet, like most attractive women, of this earth. She introduced herself and was promptly showered in a cascade of praise. "Oh!! I've heard so much about you! You are *so* beautiful. Oh my God, you are just so lovely! Jack is *so* lucky to have you!"

Christina's boyfriend Jack had run into a more subdued Marla before, at a hospital where she was holding a patient's hand. But Christina didn't know that, and she didn't know what had hit her.

Adam wanted the evening to maintain an air of composure and was afraid Marla's mania could cause a disturbance. They all sat down at the table and began engaging in a polite political discussion.

The discussion eventually meandered to the subject of the disbanded Iraqi army, which Paul Bremer of the CPA had overseen, a decision that had been hotly criticized as law and order continued to unravel and the insurgency gained strength. Adam forcefully, yet diplomatically, disagreed with Heatley, who was defending Bremer's decision.

Meanwhile, Marla was sitting next to Adam, right across from Heatley, nursing a glass of red wine and pushing food around on her plate with a fork. She was listening to their conversation like a little girl at the adults' table. She was trying to behave and keep her mouth shut. But the pain was building up inside her like lava rising to the rim of a volcano. There was so much suffering in the country, and more families were being harmed every day. So many unnecessary mistakes had been made in Iraq. She was tired of all the pain she saw on a daily basis. It wasn't right. Heatley wasn't out there holding the hands of mothers who had lost their sons, she thought.

The new Marla understood the complexities of Iraq, but the old, emotional activist began bubbling to the surface and was about to blow. She couldn't help herself.

"But what about *love*?" Marla blurted. "Aren't we all here because we *care*? Don't we all care about the people?"

Everyone stared at Marla, dumbfounded. Adam tried to contain his irritation. She was ruining it. Now Heatley would clam up.

An argument ensued, with Marla's shrillness reaching old levels. She reprimanded some misstep Heatley had made in Afghanistan and then refocused on the subject of the disastrous decision to disband the Iraqi army.

Heatley finally made a flip comment, deflecting her attack, and the storm passed. As they retreated into their respective corners, Marla's charm returned, but she was deflated, tired of all the sadness.

After dinner, the group retired to the sitting room resplendent with carpets, colorful cushions, and small Arabic tables. They smoked cigarettes, drank more wine, and continued talking.

"Hey, guys, I got ten million dollars, I can't believe it. I got ten million dollars for the families! I got ten million dollars . . . ,"

Marla trilled, trying to muster her usual enthusiasm, waving her boots and glass in the air, spilling wine on the rug.

What the hell is she talking about? Christina thought.

Although Marla didn't fully get her message across that night, she was talking about yet another success in Washington. Tim had told Marla that a dollar amount had been allocated to the Iraqi War Victims Fund created by law: ten million dollars. The total was now an astounding twenty million dollars.

By late fall, Marla was finally getting the notoriety she deserved—even if she was still desperate to get compensation for Iraqi families. Her collaboration with Human Rights Watch in Iraq had begun to turn many heads outside of media and Senate circles. Even though she didn't have an advanced degree herself, Marla was invited to speak about her work with civilian casualties of war at the Carr Center for Human Rights Policy at Harvard University's John F. Kennedy School of Government. At twenty-six years old, Marla had graduated to one of the most sacred academic chambers in the country.

Kenneth Roth, Human Rights Watch's executive director, was so impressed by her presentation at Harvard that he offered her a vacant office in their Dupont Circle Washington bureau. Changes had been made at Bobby Muller's VVAF, and to his dismay, she was no longer welcome to work there. By now she had also given up the tiny apartment on 19th Street to save money and was officially homeless. Her Human Rights Watch office became both a place to work when she was in D.C. and a storage space for her belongings. Shortly after meeting Ken, Marla tried to make an equally strong impression on one last critical individual before returning to Iraq at Thanksgiving: Aryeh Neier, president of the Open Society Institute (OSI). She had recommendations from both Tim Rieser and Ken Roth, who are people Neier takes very seriously.

Founded by billionaire George Soros, OSI is a private operations and grant-making foundation that aims to shape public policy to promote democratic governance, human rights, and economic, legal, and social reform. The prestigious foundation traditionally supports people with vast experience establishing organizations that function much more conventionally than did CIVIC. Most people would be too intimidated to even try knocking on Aryeh's door. Not Marla. If she was nervous, she disguised it under layers of effusive banter and serious rhetoric about civilian war victims in turn. CIVIC needed money to keep helping the families. The worst he could do was say no.

When Marla bounced into his New York office to talk about her work in Iraq, Aryeh was a little surprised. A former executive director of the American Civil Liberties Union and a cofounder of Human Rights Watch, he had met all kinds of characters in his day. Few, if any, were like Marla.

Then on December 2, the Open Society Institute broke its own pattern. OSI president Aryeh Neier made an exception for Marla, granting her sixty thousand dollars to keep CIVIC and its mission alive.

Chapter 13

The Battle Within

(How to Win a Soldier's Heart)

The last two years from Kabul to Baghdad, my time has been made up of rich and intimate experiences with families harmed as a result of U.S. military actions. Their tragedies are my responsibilities. I am young, and new at this and developing ways to cope, but in honesty I have tried red wine a little too much for medicine, deprived myself of sleep, and felt extremely inadequate. My life has been brightened with mentors who have covered wars from Vietnam and Central America with humanity and care. They still cry. In all of this traveling I have felt a little off base, a little lonely. So I am going to work on establishing a floor. I ask you all to remember me and that I'll be in your neck of the woods soon, and please spend time with me.
—MARLA IN HER ONLINE JOURNAL ON CIVIC'S WEBSITE,
APRIL 8, 2004

The Open Society Institute grant threw CIVIC a lifeline just in the nick of time. Marla's emotional health, however, was unraveling at a velocity that would not stop on its own. The itinerant existence, loneliness, constant exposure to suffering and violence, and her own unrelenting self-criticism ravaged her.

Marla started each morning by writing a daily "to do" list, which included how many calories, glasses of wine (usually one or two), and cigarettes (usually none) she would allow herself. The next dawn, after straying from her own instructions, she awoke in a state of self-loathing. The cycle would repeat itself almost daily. She had high hopes in the morning. By night, exhausted and traumatized, she lost some sense of self-control. She scribbled notes and wrote e-mails of apology to whomever she'd socialized with the night before. She was accustomed to lifelong swings of highs and lows, but the lows were taking over.

Her weight was the one thing Marla felt she *could* control. She hardly ever ate. When she did, she nibbled on boiled vegetables or watermelon, and picked at the Marla Salad. Her exercise routines became even more rigid. Not only had her period stopped, but her teeth were turning gray. Even two glasses of wine were too many for Marla's empty stomach and battered system.

One war zone journalist recognized symptoms of post-traumatic stress disorder (PTSD) in Marla. PTSD and alcohol dependency often go hand in hand. Marla's alcohol consumption was taking on a new dimension.

Marla passed through London in January and spent several days with Jon, who recognized signs of trauma. The latest upset had occurred on New Year's Eve, Marla's twenty-seventh birthday. A car bomb had ripped through her favorite restaurant, Nabil, where dozens of revelers were dancing and celebrating in the heavily

Christian-populated shopping district. The blast killed five Iraqis, wounded twenty-four people, including three *Los Angeles Times* reporters. Conditions in Iraq were not improving. Marla was still vibrant and fit on one level, with a cheerful persona and toned, tiny muscles. But it became clear that she might be in trouble. He'd walk downstairs in the morning and find the kitchen floor strewn with Quaker Oats after one of her midnight binges. They went out for several dinners, before which Marla promised not to drink much, but time and again, Jon had to carry her home.

"I'm sorry. I promise I'll be fine. I promise I'll be better next time," she said to Jon before she left for Baghdad.

"Marla, whatever you think about me and the life that I've led, it is actually a very destructive way of life," he told her. "Please don't seek to emulate it by spending your life running around the world without setting up a base for yourself that you can go back to, because you can't do what you're doing effectively or happily without a place to hang your hat."

Jon drove her to the airport. Marla knew that he saw other women, but she still loved him, and she wanted him to love her back. Ignoring his advice, Marla returned to Iraq to take care of civilian victims in any way she could.

Marla, Raed, and Faiz had confirmed 1,758 civilian deaths between March 20 and May 1, 2003. But the civilian death toll was escalating at a frightening rate. By early February 2004, Iraq Body Count reported that between 8,235 and 10,079 civilians had been killed since the beginning of the war—either by Coalition fire or terrorist attack. Following up with these cases by survey was impossible. Iraq had grown too dangerous, and besides, Marla and Faiz simply didn't have the resources to keep up.

Marla stepped up her collaboration with the military to help civilians. One night, Anwar Kadhum, her husband, and children unwittingly drove past a U.S. checkpoint obscured in the shadows of a dark August night when soldiers opened fire.

"Don't shoot. We are a family!" Anwar's husband yelled as the bullets began riddling the car.

Anwar's twenty-year-old son and her eighteen-year-old daughter were killed instantly. Her husband and eight-year-old daughter died from their wounds in the hospital an hour later. Without Faiz and Marla's efforts lobbying the military, Anwar, who was pregnant at the time of the shooting, most likely would have received nothing. They helped Anwar and her surviving child receive eleven thousand dollars, a small consolation for so much loss, but an acknowledgment of the tragic mistake nonetheless.

Marla had helped Tim and Senator Leahy establish through legislation the Iraqi War Victims Fund, but it was not used for military cash payments given directly to harmed civilians. The U.S. military had its own form of compensation, known as "solatia" or sympathy payments. In Iraq the payments were arbitrarily handed out to civilian victims. It was blood money. Unit commanders on the ground decided if, or how much, to compensate a family or community that was bombed or shot up—often to quell hostility. There was little impact Marla could have on facilitating these payments.

By the fall of 2003, the U.S. military had set up a handful of more formalized civilian casualty claims offices throughout

Iraq. The most central was at the Convention Center—Saddam's old palace—in the Green Zone, which provided small payments to victims who had the ability to fill out cumbersome claims forms. This, Marla thought, was something she *could* help with. After waiting for hours in a cramped office at the Convention Center, the Iraqi victims might or might not be approved for a payment. They were usually rejected, failing to provide vital information such as a death certificate, police report, photographs, and hospital records. If their house was destroyed or a relative had been buried amongst the chaos of the war, it was often nearly impossible to prove. If they did, the military afforded $2,500 for loved ones of civilians accidentally killed by U.S. firepower. The awards came from seized Iraqi funds. Marla and Faiz tapped into the program, helping scores of civilians fill out the confusing forms. While Faiz did most of the legwork, Marla stayed on top of larger issues in Baghdad.

Captain Jonathan Tracy was the judge advocate general, or JAG, in charge of the military's civilian casualty payments office in the Convention Center. Captain Tracy is fresh-faced, serious, and very well-mannered. He wears wire-rimmed glasses, has rosy cheeks, and laughs bashfully. The young army attorney's budget and reach were extremely limited, but he was sharp and well-intentioned. Like Marla, his days often left him exhausted. Marla would come to call him "My JAG," as in, "I love my JAG!"

Marla cajoled a CNN crew into producing a story about the impediments Iraqi victims faced in winning these payments from the military. She and the film crew wandered over to the Green Zone and Captain Tracy's small office stacked with boxes full of casualty and property claims files. They filmed Captain Tracy. Hopeful victims stood in a long line in the Iraqi Assistance Center, which worked in tandem with the U.S. claims office, and were patiently waiting to be screened by the center's Iraqi employees, milling around or sitting in chairs lining the walls.

The payment seekers represented a cross-section of Iraqi society. Illiterate Bedouin sheiks dressed in robes twiddled their thumbs next to slick Iraqi businessmen shouting into their cell phones. With a little luck, they would have a chance that day to speak with the JAG through Zainab, his Iraqi translator. Not wanting special treatment, Marla asked if she, too, could wait in line to talk to Captain Tracy about the process. He said that they accepted claim forms only twice a week and there were dozens of people to tend to. He suggested that she stop by his brigade quarters—in Saddam's wife's house—the next day.

She showed up when she was told, and an unofficial partnership blossomed. Captain Tracy wanted to help as many Iraqis as he could, but the task often proved difficult from his Green Zone perch. So Marla and Faiz began personally bringing forms and victims to his office for processing. They helped the Iraqis provide the required proof they needed to win the payments, traveling to communities well outside Baghdad in doing so.

Marla and her JAG forged a friendship. She adored him for working so hard to help her, Faiz, and the families. They began jogging together in the Green Zone, starting shortly after dawn to avoid the sweltering heat. She often picked his brain.

"Why is it someone like you in the army handling the claims and not someone from a government agency?" she asked Jonathan one day while they were jogging.

"Well, from my perspective, someone in uniform should offer money and an apology if it was someone in uniform who caused the damage. If I were injured or harmed, I'd at least want some representative of that organization to offer the apology. It shouldn't have to be someone coming from the outside to clean up their mess," he explained.

Christina Asquith, the *Christian Science Monitor* freelancer, willingly succumbed to Marla's pleas to write a story about Captain Tracy's claims program. In late January she spent two days in his office. She met one old, decrepit man who had been waiting for hours to tell Captain Tracy that his house had been bombed by mistake in April 2003. The impoverished farmer had brought a carefully typed list of lost belongings: one sewing machine, nine sleeping beds, ten women's dresses, one teapot, and so on. Another man, a student at Baghdad University, had been driving in an upscale neighborhood on a clothes-shopping errand when a Humvee sideswiped his car. He told Christina that he thought the soldiers, who were laughing, hit him intentionally. All he wanted was an apology. He said that he wasn't concerned with money—it was a matter of pride. Captain Tracy had his hands full.

Marla brought Bedour's case to her JAG. The eighteen-year-old's house, which was located across the street from a Baathist office in southern Iraq, was accidentally blown to bits by a U.S. bomb. She lost fourteen family members, including her mother, cousins, and uncles. Although she survived the attack, her legs and hands were badly burned. One of her hands was grossly deformed, and she could barely move her fingers.

Marla had been instrumental in convincing the United States to provide medical assistance for the girl to save her hand—and now she wanted to get her a sympathy payment as well. Marla treated Bedour as more than a claims case. She was a human being, a young girl turning into a woman. Marla looked Bedour in the eyes, touched her deformed hands with compassion, hugged her, and made her laugh.

One journalist remembers meeting Bedour shortly after she was injured. The girl was despondent and traumatized, a shadow of a human being. Months later he saw Bedour again—this time with Marla. The girl was laughing and smiling, given a new lease on life.

Marla and Christina often ran laps together around the track at Baghdad University to blow off steam. Although it was just a two-minute run from their homes, Baghdad was so dangerous that they went by car. After passing through two Iraqi checkpoints erected at the university, they stretched and began to hop around the simple asphalt track. A few Iraqi guards cradled their AK-47s, smoked cigarettes, drank tea, and watched in fascination as the two blondes passed by in their running shorts. During one of these runs, Marla admitted how hard it was getting CIVIC up and running. It was the first time Christina glimpsed the stress Marla was feeling.

On top of her running, Marla swam hundreds of laps at the Babylon Hotel's indoor pool. It was winter, so she'd given up the outdoor Hamra pool for the season. Swimming at the

Babylon, however, was risky. The hotel hosted many weddings and conferences, making it a potential terrorist target. The pool was enclosed in a glass atrium. If a bomb were to explode close by, the water would turn into a death trap. So sometimes she'd play tennis with the hotel's instructor, who used to spend his days teaching Saddam's cronies how to throw a good backswing. But most of the time, she swam. It was the only time she could truly find solace and erase the pain and stress she was feeling.

"Habibi, Habibi!" the men sang out from the pool whenever Marla arrived, calling her "darling" or "my dear" in Arabic while puffing on their cigarettes. The Iraqis didn't swim laps, but they sought solace in the pool as well. The elderly men soaked in the heavily chlorinated water, talking about the plight of their country and a time when life was worth celebrating. They represented a generation of Iraqis who came of age in the pre-Saddam 1960s, when Iraq experienced a brief spell of democracy and the Tigris was lined with cosmopolitan restaurants.

Marla jumped into the pool in her funky bathing suit that was three sizes too big, hanging off her little body. Before shooting off for an hourlong swim, she greeted the men effusively and took the time to talk to them, asking about their dreams and bringing them a moment of peace.

In early February the sympathy payments piece featuring Marla and her JAG aired on CNN International. Proud of the success, Marla wrote home to a long list of friends and colleagues. She was enjoying parties and friends, she said, which was only true to an extent. She was still pretending that everything was okay.

In reality, Marla had finally come to recognize that she was not well. She had seen a psychiatrist in Amman a few months before, who put her on antidepressant medication. She had been sitting in an empty hotel room between one of her many trips traveling between Baghdad and Washington, when she was overcome by a debilitating sense of loneliness and depression. The wild highs and lows she'd experienced all her life were beginning to make sense: There was something wrong. Her twin brother Mark had been diagnosed with bipolar disorder—more commonly known as manic depression—when he was just nineteen years old. Maybe she had a chemical imbalance as well. Compounding that—whether she recognized it yet or not—was the grinding trauma produced by the circumstances of her daily life.

Marla began opening up to friends such as Cat Philp, the Scottish *Times* of London journalist, slowly coming out of the closet about her emotional and psychological struggles. By late February, Cat was due to return to her home base in New Dehli, and Marla was afflicted with separation anxiety. Accompanying Cat as far as Amman for a few day's rest, she visited her psychiatrist again. The antidepressant medication didn't seem to be working, she told the doctor. The stress was also causing her skin to break out, and another doctor wrote her a prescription for an acne medication, which contraindicated the antidepressant, only confusing her system more. Further complicating things was the red wine. Antidepressants amplify the impact of alcohol—a depressant itself. Conversely, alcohol diminishes the effects of antidepressants. It was a vicious cycle.

Tara Sutton, a long-legged and striking brunette from

Canada in her midthirties, spent blocks of time in Baghdad rather than staying on continuously. Many journalists rotated in and out to give themselves time to decompress or cover stories outside of Iraq. Her earlier memories of Marla were of a bubbly ray of sunshine that glided around Baghdad in a blue sundress and a chic head scarf.

When Tara returned to Baghdad in March 2004, Marla appeared very different. She was now living with Tara's then-boyfriend and fellow Canadian Patrick Graham and British journalist Rory McCarthy. At Marla's request, Tara stocked up on "chick" magazines at the airport. Upon delivery, she pored over *Glamour*, *Elle*, and *Cosmopolitan*, hungry for health and beauty tips.

Most of the time, Marla was light and enthusiastic at the house. Patrick and Tara nicknamed her nighttime alter ego "Honey Nut" because she razed through their boxes of Cheerios after hours. In the morning, they discovered that all the cabinets were open and everything was sticky with honey. They could track her movements by her handprints.

Tara became Marla's new closest friend in Baghdad, as well as her caretaker. Marla went out every night, sometimes hitting three parties or dinners in a row. She never did much eating, though. She'd return home late, often upset, usually after too much wine. Tara put her to bed, and Marla began opening up.

"You're so lucky you have Patrick, Tara. I wish I had someone like that. I love you so much, thank you for listening. I'm so glad you take care of me . . . ," Marla told her over and over again before she would fall into a deep slumber.

One night Marla was aching to go out, but Tara made it her mission to keep her indoors.

"Just stay in with us, babe, and chill out. We'll have a fun mellow night," Tara said. Marla lay down on the couch and put her head in her friend's lap. Tara began stroking Marla's hair. Her breath smelled like honey, which she'd just eaten straight out of the jar.

"Nobody loves me. Why doesn't anybody love me? You're so beautiful and you have so many friends. Will you always be my friend?"

"Calm down, calm down," Tara cooed, continuing to stroke her hair. "What are you talking about? Everybody loves you, Marla. Of course I'll always be your friend."

Road to Recovery

(How to Heal the Wounds)

I am feeling like I will change. I went for a walk today and real-
ized how much more people will love me and how much better
I will be when I am well—when I don't have to worry about all
my screw ups, being thin. In my head I will be so much better
of a person and CIVIC will be better too. Life will start.
— MARLA IN AN E-MAIL TO HER FRIEND
CAT PHILP, JULY 2004

Marla knew she had to leave Iraq. She was
finally beginning to admit to herself, and to others, that she
needed to heal her own wounds. But she vacillated between
clarity and denial. Marla went to Thailand for two weeks' rest
and then returned to Amman. She hadn't talked to Jon in
months and called him, confessing that she was "ill" and was
returning to Baghdad for just a few days.

Violence in Iraq was spiraling out of control, and foreigners
were increasingly under threat of abductions and beheadings.

The siege of Fallujah had gripped the country while Marla was away, and civilian bloodshed was rising. Many journalists in Iraq were now living under virtual house arrest, abandoning their rented homes for the safety of the Hamra. Jon and other friends were concerned about Marla's plans to return. Not only was it dangerous, but her stability was deteriorating rapidly. Peter Bergen sent her an e-mail on April 14 while she was still in Amman:

> *Marla, please stay safe in Baghdad. I have been a little concerned about your drinking. . . . It's a big problem on a lot of levels. I think this will damage everything you have been creating if it continues, not just personally, but also CIVIC and its mission.*
>
> *So I really think you need to address this problem. I know that you are under a lot of pressure in Iraq, but you have to think about yourself. . . .*
>
> *Marla, you might also want to think about getting a permanent base somewhere in the US. This constantly moving can't be good psychologically . . . just a thought. . . . love P*

Against everyone's wishes, Marla returned to Iraq. She moved into the new suite at the Hamra where Christina Asquith and her boyfriend Jack Fairweather were living. She was stuck there—unable to go to the Babylon for her swims, unable to jog in the Green Zone. She ventured out now and again with Faiz, but it was risky. Nonetheless, she always found new projects to take on. Hundreds of civilians had been killed in Fallujah, many of them women and children. Although Marla didn't travel to the city, she stretched her three days in Baghdad into two weeks. She wanted to concentrate on finding a way to assess the human cost in Fallujah—in addition to lobbying the military to award more sympathy payments to families she identified in her survey.

To her family and friends' relief Marla finally left Iraq in early May. She made a very quick stop in London, and despite her better judgment, stayed with Jon. He couldn't give her the love she wanted, but she was always forgiving and again agreed to be friends. She met Cat in New York, where they lit up Manhattan with Quil and other journalists they knew from Baghdad. Quil invited Marla to a cocktail reception hosted by the Ploughshares Fund, a public grant-making foundation. She was sticking to her new "one glass of wine" policy, bouncing around the room charming total strangers and making important contacts. Quil and Marla then dashed downtown to a gallery opening, where she had another glass of wine or two. By the time they sat down to dinner with Cat, Marla's charisma had turned into an almost wildly psychedelic version of itself. It was like a bad Marla trip, as opposed to the normal good one. The switch seemed to happen instantly.

After a few days in New York, Cat and Marla were due to travel to California. At the last minute, Marla got word that Peter Bergen was throwing one of his famous parties. Quickly changing plans, Marla dragged Cat on a detour through Washington.

* * *

A few months earlier, I had decided to take a break from my press job at the United Nations World Food Program to try freelance writing. The first article idea that popped into my head was Marla. We'd exchanged occasional e-mails since I'd last seen her in San Francisco in the summer of 2002. I was amazed by the progress she had made in Washington and Iraq and thought her story would be an easy sell to a women's magazine. I had never written for one before, but an editor at *Elle* bought the pitch. Marla was thrilled when I told her in late March. I wanted to travel to Baghdad in mid-April to report the story, and we began discussing plans.

Little did we know that by April 18, traveling to Iraq would be foolhardy at best. At the magazine's urging, I canceled my plans. I was relieved but didn't want to give up on the story, persuading my editor that it would still work if I interviewed Marla in San Francisco instead. *Elle* was dubious but told me to give it a try. The only problem was, by the time Marla was due in San Francisco in early May, I would only have a few days to make my deadline. After reading an e-mail from Marla informing me of her change of plans, I landed in San Francisco from my base in South Africa and caught a red-eye to Washington.

I heard Marla before I saw her. We were meeting at the Human Rights Watch offices in Dupont Circle, and as I sat in the reception area, a flood of booming chatter and laughter spilled into the room. A moment later Marla appeared, looking radiant. She had much shorter hair and seemed thinner, but it had been so long since I'd seen her that it didn't strike me as out of the ordinary. She whisked me into her office. It was piled high with suitcases, boxes, half-read books, loose folders, and, somewhere in there, a computer. She shot off a few e-mails, babbling all the while. Over the next few hours, I ran to keep up with the fast pace of the Marla-guided tour of the capital. Our first appointment was at the Open Society Institute's Washington branch. Marla sat down in the conference room with a female OSI employee, and I joined them. When she opened her mouth and launched into a briefing on the inner workings of Iraq, I realized this was not the carefree, ditzy Marla I knew. The person before me was a rock-solid human rights advocate.

After leaving, we ducked into a market, where she bought a bag of chips. "See, this is all I eat, I don't have time for lunch!" Then she dashed out into the street to hail us a cab. Our next stop was the Senate.

From the comfort of a floppy couch, I listened to Marla and Tim brainstorm as Donald Rumsfeld talked on a small TV screen above their heads. I was surprised by the run-down, dated look of the office.

"I want to get the State Department to create a civilian casualties desk," Marla said to Tim, suggesting that war victims warranted a permanent government office to address their grievances. Marla's grand scheme was not to keep doing the job herself—the end goal was to convince the government or military that it was their job and for them to take over with a systematic process.

"I don't know. I think the Department of Defense may be the best place to try," Tim replied, "They're the ones responsible."

They continued talking for a while, and then we were off again. She had to meet Cat. I was exhausted and returned to my hotel for a nap.

After postponing our sit-down interview several times, Marla finally met me at Starbucks the next day. She'd had a two-hour swim and a champagne lunch, which caused her to be delayed. We sat out on the patio and began talking. She had difficulty focusing on my questions and was growing impatient. It finally occurred to me that she was a little drunk and distracted. But there was more to it.

She apologized for being so out of it—that she was "sick." I didn't know exactly what she meant, but I had a hunch that it was psychological and that perhaps she was traumatized from Iraq. She wept uncontrollably. And then, like an afternoon storm, the rain was gone, replaced by sunshine.

We talked about her childhood and her work. She told me she wanted to "find a good dude" and mentioned more than once that she wished she were prettier. I was puzzled by the comment, not only because in Afghanistan she had come across as boldly confident and carefree, but clearly her value as a woman and a human being transcended looks. I was also baffled because she was a perky blonde who attracted a lot of male attention. She said casually that her twin brother was "the good-looking one."

We left Starbucks and started walking to Tim's house a

few blocks away, where she was staying. "Isn't it a beautiful day?" she chirped to everyone we passed.

At Tim's I met Cat. She was quiet. In retrospect I realized she must have been worried. Marla handed me a crumpled note she'd scrawled out on a piece of notebook paper earlier that said something along the lines of "Thanks, Jen, you rock! XXX Marla."

The next night I went to the party at Peter Bergen's house, where Marla and Cat were busy socializing. Marla seemed to be in much better shape than the day before. I stayed for several hours but left before the night was over. I had an early flight the next morning to Oakland.

"Marla Ruzicka, Marla Ruzicka, please pick up a white courtesy phone."

Nancy and Cliff were waiting out front and had made the call to the airport to alert Marla. I had just arrived at the airport in Oakland, California, on another flight and was surprised to hear the announcement and then see Marla and Cat waiting for their suitcases next to the baggage carousel. I promised to update her on the *Elle* article and we said good-bye.

It was Mother's Day and Nancy and Marla greeted each other brightly. Next they picked up Mark, who had been attending an AA meeting halfway between Oakland and Lakeport. It was a wild ride. Mark took over at the wheel, and Marla thought he was driving much too fast and much too recklessly, whipping around the turns, hugging the mountain roads. Cat had been in a car accident in Iraq the year before, and Marla was hypersensitive to her feelings.

Marla hollered for him to slow down. Mark, however, said he was driving fine and that Marla was exaggerating. They began bickering.

Cat and Marla spent a day in Lakeport and then drove in the protest-mobile three hours south back to San Francisco. Cat was growing weary. While Marla was driving, Cat finally mustered the courage, in Marla lingo, "to kick her ass."

They descended into the Napa Valley and Cat let loose.

"You've got to get help. You can't go on like this," Cat said.

"What are you talking about?" Marla asked.

"Look, it's the drinking, and your mind's not functioning straight. You're changing plans every two seconds. You really seem out of control, and you need to get a handle on things. You're not eating. You've got to start taking care of yourself. . . ."

Marla listened quietly, nodding her head. She had already admitted to Cat that she suffered from depression and knew she had to cut back on drinking. She finally fessed up to her eating disorder as well.

"You're right, you're right, Cat," she finally said, telling her about Fran, a psychologist she knew in Lakeport who had counseled her when she was younger. Marla picked up her cell phone and in seconds was talking to Fran. She told her that she might be bipolar like her brother and wanted to make an appointment.

"Oh, honey, we did always wonder if you were bipolar," Fran said. "Yes, come and see me."

They arrived in San Francisco and checked into a posh Nob Hill hotel. Marla wanted to keep it social as usual, but then realized she wasn't as connected to the old circle as she used to be.

"I could introduce you to all my activist friends, but most of them don't speak with me anymore," she said to Cat. She and Medea, her old mentor, barely talked.

Marla showed Cat the town. They walked up and down the Haight-Ashbury neighborhood and bought wacky clothes and went to a bar tended by drag queens. They were drinking the same amount, but the effect on Marla was much stronger. Before Cat could cut her off, Marla started hopping around the bar, clapping her hands to the music, beckoning everyone to join in.

"Oh, honey, you've had enough to drink!" one drag queen said to Marla in a deep voice.

"You have such great tits!" Marla responded, laughing.

Cat took Marla to nice restaurants, forcing her to eat. When they passed through Napa Valley, they stopped at the Culinary Institute of America, where Cat pointed out enticing canapés. Marla once admitted to Cat that anorexia had been "her only real friend."

"Wow, I haven't looked at food like this in so long," Marla said, popping a canapé into her mouth.

Cat returned to New Delhi soon after that, but she asked Marla to promise that she would see Fran and get better. Marla said she would. Marla went back to Lakeport and kept the appointment with Fran. She also met with a doctor and began working on her eating disorder. But she grew restless and craved to flee her own demons. Convincing herself she was better, Marla boarded a plane and returned to Iraq.

✿ ✿ ✿

Marla returned to Baghdad a week before the transition of power from the Coalition Provisional Authority to the Iraqi interim government on June 30, 2004. She attended a VIP ceremony marking the historical moment, but the highlight of her visit was being back in the business of interacting with Iraqi civilians. It reenergized Marla, yet she was concerned about safety. After two weeks, Marla retreated into Cat's care in New Delhi, leaving Faiz to run CIVIC in Iraq. Instead of returning to California to get back into her treatment program, Marla was planning to hop over to Kabul next. She hadn't been back for nearly two years and she needed to follow up on civilian casualties there, she said. Cat put her foot down and practically dragged her to the airport to catch a plane home.

Back in Lakeport, Marla was officially diagnosed with low-grade bipolar disorder and began experimenting with lithium, a medication prescribed to counter the effects of the chemical imbalance. In many ways, the diagnosis itself gave Marla some peace of mind. It explained the uncontrollable swings of mood and emotion she had experienced her entire life.

The energizing highs that fueled her grandiose ambitions and debilitating lows that crippled her emotionally were finally beginning to make sense. Marla wanted to get better. She could get back to caring for others as soon as she was healthy and emotionally stable but her struggles were layered.

Like post-traumatic stress disorder, bipolar disorder goes hand in hand with substance abuse. It is an incapacitating symptom of the disease. The trauma of Iraq and the reality of her illness played off each other in cruel and harmful ways. Anorexia was a symptom of that. But Marla was giving it her all to break the self-destructive cycle.

Marla spent July and August of 2004 in Lakeport, visiting with her parents; her godmother, Eileen McGuire; and her therapist, Fran. She went wake-boarding and took long swims. She cut back on her drinking almost completely and started an outpatient eating program in nearby Santa Rosa. Four days a week, she woke up early and drove west on the winding country roads, returning to Lakeport in the afternoons.

Facing her illness wasn't easy, but Marla enjoyed spending time with her family, whom she hadn't seen much of in years. She also relished eating salmon, which she said "grew on trees" at her parent's house. For the first time in ages, Marla and her brother Mark were getting along. She confided in him about her problems, asking him questions about bipolar disorder and crying on his shoulder.

In September 2004, after nearly two months in Lakeport, Marla returned to Washington, staying with friends again. She had gained weight, was taking her medication, and felt it was time to slowly venture out into the world again. The lithium sapped her of some of her energy, which she missed, but she stuck with the program.

Searching for ways to keep on top of her work from the United States, she even traveled to Fort Stewart in Georgia, home of the U.S. Army's 3rd Infantry Division. She led a civilian casualty sensitivity seminar in October for soldiers who were scheduled to be deployed to Iraq. In between projects, she occasionally slipped up, drinking more than one glass of wine, but rebounded the next morning, determined to be strong.

In November, Marla took the advice of her friends Cat, Jon, and Peter and finally established a home base. She wanted a fresh start. Although she visited often to work with Tim and see a new therapist, she left D.C. and its claustrophobic social circles, which tempted her to drink. Instead of rushing back to the war zone, which also tempted her, she moved to New York, subletting a room in a friend's apartment in the East Village.

Cat landed in New York the week before Thanksgiving to visit friends. Marla tumbled into JFK, anxious to hug her friend as soon as she set foot on U.S. soil. She arrived late, and Cat couldn't get through to her on her cell phone (she often left it in the backseats of taxicabs) but was delighted when she finally showed up. She was thrilled to see that Marla had gained at least twenty pounds. In Manhattan they met up with another friend and drank champagne, but Marla held herself together. Cat was impressed by how much self-discipline Marla was exercising—even if it was for her benefit. They went shopping in Soho. She saw a dress on sale that she liked at a funky boutique for a hundred dollars and tried it on.

"What do you think of this? Hideous? Oooooh! I really like it, it's so cute, Cat! But I don't know if I should. That's a lot of money. I've never paid that much for clothes before."

Cat encouraged Marla to treat herself, and she splurged.

Overall, Cat was pleased to see how much improvement Marla had made, but she was still in the process of recovering. After finishing up some shopping in midtown one day, Marla told Cat to walk ahead of her for a while. She needed to call her psychologist. Marla had an emergency therapy session on her cell phone as she walked through Times Square.

Nancy and Marla spent a few days over Thanksgiving in a Yucatan resort relaxing. It was packed with couples and Marla joined a group of lovebirds relaxing in a hot tub by the pool.

"How many of you are on your honeymoon?"

Several arms shot in the air.

"How many of you are here with your mothers?"

Marla waved her hand in the air, eliciting a round of laughter.

In the evenings they ate Marla's favorite seafood, and one night they *both* had too much to drink at the hotel's rooftop restaurant and began talking about the men in Marla's life.

"Mom, there's something I never told you: I got married on my lunch break right after Phillip moved to San Francisco!"

Nancy was shocked, to say the least. They squawked like two chickens as they drank their wine. Marla loved Phillip and they remained extremely close, she said, but they had grown apart romantically and were now irreversibly leading separate lives. It was time to start thinking about making it official. They also talked about Marla's recovery. Nancy seemed a bit frustrated that Marla wasn't altogether well yet. Like her daughter, she was a fast mover who could be impatient. Nancy figured that Marla must be strong enough to get better if she could function in Iraq, compared to Mark, who she often coddled and whose bipolar lows were immobilizing. Marla tried to make her mom understand that, just like Mark, she also needed some time and care.

Back in New York, the Open Society Institute offered her a free desk in their headquarters, where she was looking forward to making friends and networking.

Despite her efforts to make friends and think positively about herself, Marla was depressed and lonely again. Cat was gone, and she didn't have very many friends in New York. She was trying to stay positive but was battling to find a place to focus her energies other than fund-raising. She had lunch with Sam from Human Rights Watch, whose office was near hers, in the Empire State Building. They had become fairly good friends since her days in Kabul. Marla told him she was feeling down, asking him, "Why do men suck?" She also asked for career advice. She wanted to get back to Iraq. He strongly opposed the idea. It was too dangerous for her kind of work, which required moving around Baghdad and beyond. So he concocted the perfect diversion.

Nepal was fresh territory and much less dangerous for foreigners than Iraq. A civil war was under way between the ruling monarchy's forces and Maoist rebels. Civilians were trapped in the middle. Both sides were guilty of human rights abuses, but the United States was still providing military aid to the monarchists, which Human Rights Watch disapproved of. Not enough was being done to document the abuses, and Sam wanted to raise the war's profile in the media. He thought Marla would be the perfect person to carry out a fact-finding mission and bring international attention to the war. Marla could again play the good cop to Human Rights Watch's bad cop.

On December 22, Cat picked Marla up at the airport in New Delhi, and they had a happy reunion. On Christmas Eve, Cat threw a party at her house. Busy entertaining other guests, she hadn't noticed that Marla was drinking too much until she started to wobble and spill wine. Cat tried to convince her to go to sleep, but she refused. So she locked Marla in the bedroom. A few minutes later, she reappeared. She had climbed out the window to rejoin the party. In the morning, she was mortified to learn that she'd ruined Cat's carpets and apologized profusely. They went to a friend's house for Christmas Day lunch and Marla behaved, enchanting the other guests with her screwball humor. The tsunami hit Southeast Asia the next day. Cat rushed off to Sri Lanka and Marla flew to Nepal. Before diving into the human rights crisis, she went on a trek in the Himalayas.

Returning from her trek, she knocked on doors in Katmandu, which opened wide to her disarming personality. As Sam suspected, Marla had scoped out the human rights community within days of her arrival. She made friends fast. The government was arresting human rights workers and she wanted to find a way to protect them, a challenge she'd never taken on before. She met with officials at the U.S. embassy and documented cases of civilian abuse. In a note to friends, she wrote that she was not against U.S. military aid to the

Nepalese Army—as long as they respected human rights. Marla began pitching the Nepal story to her old Kabul and Baghdad journalist contacts.

Marla tried to convince herself that Nepal could be a good substitute for Iraq. Although she was energized by the experience, it didn't have quite the same pull as Baghdad. To keep herself distracted, she returned to Kabul. She was elated to be back.

Afghanistan loved her, too. Everywhere Marla went, she was greeted with beaming smiles. As she walked or jogged the street, Afghans called out to her from opened windows: "Marla Jan," Marla, my friend. She was reunited with Arifa, the woman who had tried to deliver a letter to the U.S. Embassy after her husband was killed by a bomb. She noticed that Kabul had changed a bit and was surprised to see how many bars had opened there. But its soul was unaltered and Marla was happy again.

Marla sought out the U.S. military in Kabul, which was starting to deliver sympathy payments to Afghan civilians as it was doing in Iraq. She planned on returning at a later date to work with them. At Tim's urging, she also checked up on the community reconstruction assistance that legislation had outlined back in August 2002. The International Organization for Migration, an agency that works with refugees and displaced populations, was administering the aid. More work needed to be done, but some progress was being made in pockets of eastern Afghanistan. She wanted to continue monitoring the program—something that was too dangerous for her to undertake in Iraq.

Marla was also reunited with some foreigners who were still based in Kabul. One of them was an English woman she had been friendly with in 2002. They sat down to have a chat and gossip one day. She was also friends with Jon Swain. Marla learned things in the course of that conversation that broke her heart. It turned out that Jon had been to Italy with the English woman in May of 2003, which is when, according to Marla, he had promised *her* a holiday from the stress of Baghdad. He had told her that he was in South Africa visiting his son at the time. There were other lies as well. More than anything, Marla was inconsolably hurt that he had been so dishonest with her. Marla struggled to understand that the rejection was not her fault—that it was not a result of her not being good enough or pretty enough.

Cat met Marla, laden with new Afghan vests, at the baggage carousel at the airport in New Delhi in mid-January 2005. Despite the upsetting news from her English friend, she was on a high from the trip to Afghanistan. Over the next few days, she fought to stay positive and not let the Jon disappointment drag her down—but it was hard. One day Cat was concerned that Marla would falter at dinner at the Imperial Hotel. Although she was teetering on the edge of another manic episode, she managed to keep Cat's group of friends well entertained, regaling them with gut-splitting tales about hugging soldiers in Iraq.

"Do you need a hug too?" she asked Cat's friends. "These are the only arms that Fallujah needs!" The more they laughed, the further she'd go.

On January 20, Marla was leafing through Cat's newspaper, the *Times* of London, when she came upon a double-page spread about U.S. soldiers who had unknowingly shot up a car full of civilians—the Hassan family—in Iraq.

"Oh my God! Look, Cat! Have you read this?"

"Yeah, it's awful, the kids' parents were killed," she said, glancing over.

"No, no, not that part. It says here that the military filled out *forms* about the incident!" she said and started scribbling something in her notebook. "Can I keep this?"

An American photojournalist Marla knew, Chris Hondros, had witnessed the shoot-up in the town of Tal Afar in northern Iraq. He had joined a group of soldiers based a short distance outside of town on a spontaneous night patrol.

Just after six p.m. on January 18, a few minutes after curfew, the unit descended from its armored vehicles and began walking the dark, deserted streets, their weapons at the ready. About five minutes later, a car turned onto the boulevard. The soldiers were dressed in camouflage, and there were no streetlights. They fired three shots in the air as a warning. The car sped up, its driver clearly frightened. The soldiers were frightened too, worried that it might be a suicide bomber, and riddled the windshield with bullets. It rolled to a stop at the intersection. Six children tumbled out of the backseat, screaming in terror, soaked in their parents' blood. Their mother and father were mangled in the front seat, dead.

The soldiers ran toward the car when they realized what had happened. Chris began taking photographs. The soldiers scooped up the children and carried them to the sidewalk to inspect them for wounds. They were nicked from broken glass, but otherwise seemed to be intact, and the soldiers bound up their injuries before rushing them to the local hospital. They towed the car over as well. The kids were whisked away while their parents were carried to the hospital in body bags. After being examined, it turned out that one boy, Rakan, had been shot through the stomach, and the doctors saved him. Everyone in the patrol, including Chris, had to make sworn statements about the incident once back on base. He filled out his form describing what he had seen.

What Chris witnessed, and recorded, was a small but extremely important fact. One of Marla's main goals had been to push the military to conduct their own civilian casualty count for compensation purposes. The military had repeatedly denied that it maintained records of Iraqis harmed or killed by U.S firepower. Here was the proof that they did.

Marla packed her suitcase, tucked the newspaper into her laptop bag, and returned to New York.

Last Rites

Just a quick note, to say that Faiz [who runs CIVIC in Iraq] and I are safe. Today, there were some car bombs that exploded close to where I stay but we are very much protected in the compound where I live.

I will leave early next week. It will be hard because we are doing tremendous work and solving many problems.
—MARLA IN AN E-MAIL TO FAMILY AND FRIENDS,
APRIL 14, 2005

Marla looked as if she'd taken a wrong turn some-where, accidentally ending up in an East Village bistro instead of a Mongolian yurt. She breezed into the restaurant that late-January evening wearing a new Afghan vest with a scraggly collar made of shorn goat fur. Platinum hair extensions streamed out from under a bulky fur hat. It was something more fitting for a Russian czar than a California urchin. But somehow she pulled it off. She clunked over in her black boots and gave me a hug and then flirtatiously asked the bartender for a free tasting of their wine selection before she ordered a glass. "That's how you drink for free," she whispered to me when his back was turned. She looked great; like Cat, I was amazed by how much weight she had gained in such a short amount of time. Her figure was attractive and curvy. Her spirits seemed to be high after the trip to Afghanistan.

Marla and I decided to concentrate full-time on completing a book proposal and, hopefully, writing the book during the next few months. She had asked me to cowrite a memoir about her work with families of civilian casualties, and I agreed. I quit my latest UN job in Sudan and sublet an apartment in Brooklyn in order to facilitate our collaboration. So there we were, together in New York City, nursing a couple of broken hearts and trying to refocus our respective lives after years of ricocheting around the world.

The book was something positive to concentrate on, Marla said, and she was ready to sit down and start doing long interviews. She told me how happy her mom was that she had appeared in the pages of *Elle*. Marla even asked for my editor's contact information; she wanted to ask for a free makeover. I didn't realize how significant the book project was to Marla. She needed another distraction from returning to Iraq and a project to lift her self-esteem. The only problem was that writing requires patience and isolation. It wasn't an activity she could hurry along by making phone calls and rushing around. Compared to what she was used to, it was a dull, sedentary job.

We met at a Brooklyn café and discussed the contents of the proposal, and I asked her tedious questions about her life. She was wearing her fur hat and vest again, with a mismatched sweatsuit on underneath. Her hair extensions were tangled in knots. Marla told Iraq stories in her loud California voice. I wondered what she sounded like to the bookish Brooklynites in the cafe.

After the interviewing was completed, Marla had to wait for me to finish writing the proposal. Then she would have to patiently stand by while publishers read it. She wasn't good at waiting. So she began distracting herself in other ways.

Marla went to her office at OSI every day, keeping in contact with her wide network of friends and colleagues by phone and e-mail. She Rollerbladed from her apartment in the East Village to her office on West 59th Street and went on jogs along the Hudson River. She saw two therapists, once a week each. She wanted to apply for grants but had difficulty articulating her ambitions into narrative form. She kept her finger on the pulse of the civilian casualty issue in Iraq and was in regular contact with Faiz, who braved the risks in Baghdad to keep CIVIC alive.

On February 3, Marla heard a very disturbing sound bite on CNN. On the advice of Human Rights Watch's military analyst, Marc Garlasco, she wrote a letter to the *New York Times* editor, which ran on February 5, 2005:

To the Editor:

Lt. Gen. James N. Mattis's comments during a speech in San Diego, remarking that "it's fun to shoot some people," in reference to the wars in Iraq and Afghanistan, are appalling. At a time when the United States military is trying to win hearts and minds in both countries, and when Iraqis think that American forces are trigger-happy, his words are counterproductive. For our troops who are dying every day, making war sound like a sport is beyond distasteful.

General Mattis was defended by Gen. Michael W. Hagee, who said that "he intended to reflect the unfortunate and harsh realities of war." From living in Afghanistan and Iraq for much of the last three years, assisting noncombatants harmed in the crossfire, I find that General Mattis's comments do not represent what it is like to lose a loved one or a home. For a parent in the United States who lost a brave young son or daughter, his words are far from comforting.

I have worked with many of our servicemen who have helped me assist innocent civilians injured accidentally by American forces. It is not fair that their acts of kindness and care are misrepresented by General Mattis's undignified remarks.

Marla Ruzicka

New York, Feb. 4, 2005

The writer is founder, Campaign for Innocent Victims in Conflict.

Shortly after she submitted this letter, one of Marla's acquaintances in Iraq contacted her regarding an unreported story about former female Iraqi inmates who had allegedly been abused by the U.S. military at the infamous Abu Ghraib prison south of Baghdad. Marla called Sam and suggested that Human Rights Watch look into the allegations, but they didn't have anyone available at the time. Marla volunteered. Sam suggested that the sources travel to Jordan to meet with Marla, rather than her going into Iraq. But she couldn't resist.

During a second conversation with Sam, Marla came up with another idea.

"I can go into Iraq and it will be totally fine. I'll have the women come to me at the Hamra. I won't even have to leave the hotel. What do you think?"

"I don't think much of the idea," Sam said. Nobody liked the idea that Marla was returning to Iraq. Many friends and colleagues tried to dissuade her. But she was definitely already set. She was going. It was a question of how to do it safely.

Sam and Marla called a *60 Minutes* producer, who expressed interest in covering the story. After they hung up, he turned to Marla.

"I think you should let *60 Minutes* do all the hard work, and you can act as their liaison," he said.

After that conversation, she forged ahead, making plans to uncover the story herself, with or without *60 Minutes* on board. Sam noticed a difference in Marla. She was happier.

Marla also wanted to follow up on the Tal Afar incident, which proved that the military kept records of civilian casualties. She had held on to the *Times* of London article with Chris Hondros's spread that she'd picked up at Cat's apartment in New Delhi.

An additional bonus was that Cat would be in Baghdad.

Marla was excited—but also anxious. She was well aware of how dangerous Iraq had become.

Marla had dinner with Chris Hondros and two other journalists in an Italian restaurant in the East Village. They told her Rakan, the boy who had been shot through the belly, had been saved; but he was not well. The bullet was still lodged in the orphan's spine. Sophisticated surgery that couldn't be found in Iraq was required to remove it. If it wasn't, he might never walk again.

By the time I arrived, the group had already polished off their meals, but Marla was still hatching plans on how to evacuate Rakan to an appropriate hospital. It was only the second or third time I had witnessed Marla operating in full manic work mode. Chris listened, calmly interjecting his own thoughts and ideas. A few minutes later, manic Marla faded away to be replaced by bubbly Marla. As we left the restaurant, she greeted other patrons on their way in.

"Happy St. Patrick's Day! Happy St. Patrick's Day!"

Marla and I went to a nearby wine bar for a private chat. We gossiped and finished our drinks, then walked out onto Second Avenue. I wished Marla luck in Iraq, imploring her to take care, and with a wave good-bye she bounced away toward her apartment. It was the last time I ever saw her.

Marla landed in "Baggers," as she called it, on March 23. Arriving at the now fortified Hamra Hotel, she bounded upstairs and into Cat's room.

"Yaaaaayyyy! Cat, I'm here!!!" she squealed, hugging her friend. She saw Cat's driver—Faiz's brother—and began hugging and kissing him as well. It wasn't exactly orthodox to greet a man in such a way in Iraq, and he blushed with discomfort. Marla was unfazed. She was finally home.

After they caught up, Cat suggested that Marla stay in her suite. Thanking her for the offer, Marla declined, explaining that the Ford Foundation had given her a five-thousand-dollar travel grant for the trip. She would be interviewing Iraqi women and needed privacy.

When they weren't working, Cat and Marla spent all their time together. Marla noticed that the Hamra scene was dull compared to her last trip and that most of the journalists she knew were gone. But that was fine; she had plenty of work and wanted as much alone time with Cat as possible. Instead of lavishing all the gifts she'd brought for Cat all at once, each morning Marla left a single present, accompanied by a loving note, in front of her door: a bag of chocolates, French vanilla coffee, a *New Yorker* magazine, *People*, and even Thai cooking ingredients. Every morning Cat opened her hotel door to one of her drivers holding Marla's bag of goodies and looking puzzled.

Marla quickly got down to business, attacking projects with her old ferocity. She reunited with Faiz and gave him warm congratulations—and plenty of hugs. His wife had given birth to their first child, a little girl, in February. In Marla's absence, Faiz had kept CIVIC running, working to get sympathy payments for the war victims. But for the next two weeks, they had a new priority. They connected with an Iraqi journalist who knew where to find the former Iraqi women prisoners who had allegedly been abused. It was a very sensitive issue, and many of them were afraid to talk.

A local journalist had lined up a string of other sources who had information about the abuse claims, but Marla wasn't sure if she trusted them. During her first few days in Baghdad, many characters, some unseemly, streamed in and out of Marla's hotel room.

One afternoon Faiz and Marla burst into Cat's room, racked with nervous giggles. Faiz joked that he needed a drink.

"What's going on with you two?" Cat asked.

"We just interviewed one of the famous torture victims," she said, referring to one of the Iraqi prisoners whom U.S. soldiers had photographed at Abu Ghraib.

"Cat, he was really freaking me out. He kept saying how much he hates America. What am I going to do? Oh my God, Cat, this scary dude was in my room and knows where I *live*."

Cat calmed them down, helping them laugh off the harrowing experience. After Faiz left, Cat took a more serious tone. She was worried, and so was Marla. She wasn't stupid and knew that people who end up in Abu Ghraib are no angels.

A day or two later, Marla knocked on Cat's door at about six p.m. They walked out onto her balcony and had another discussion. Marla had just interviewed a woman who claimed to have been abused. But there was something about the woman's story she didn't trust. She felt the pressure to deliver to *60 Minutes* but just didn't feel she was receiving credible information.

"You know what to do, Marla. Don't let someone bully you into something when your integrity's on the line. It's not a smoking gun kind of thing. You don't have to do it."

"I know, I know. You're totally right and Tim said the same thing. I don't want to let them down, but if the story's not there, I guess it's just not."

Cat was due to leave Iraq in late March. Marla planned to stay on for another week, and Cat wanted to make sure she was well looked after. In the days before she departed, she introduced Marla to as many of the new faces as possible. Marla didn't mind: Most of her old friends were gone, so she'd just make new ones. A few familiar faces were still around, such as *Christian Science Monitor* freelancer Jill Carroll and *New York Times* journalist Edward Wong, who she knew from her previous trips to Iraq. One night Cat took her to a party at the *Washington Post/Chicago Tribune* house, next door to the Hamra. There she met a friend of Cat's, Colin McMahon, a reporter for the *Chicago Tribune*, and they got along well. She also hit it off with Ellen Knickmeyer and Caryl Murphy of the *Washington Post* bureau and began eating dinner at the house regularly.

Every morning, Marla wheedled her way into the NBC bureau's gym and then returned to the Hamra after a good workout, charging into Cat's room, giddy from an endorphin buzz. The morning Cat was due to leave was like any other. Marla bounced over to Cat, ready to tackle the day. After a few moments, she was gripped by sadness and bolted up.

"I have to leave now, before I start crying," she said to Cat, embracing her tightly. And then she was gone.

Marla soon abandoned the Abu Ghraib project altogether and began focusing on more pressing matters. Slowly, she began to venture out onto Baghdad's streets with Faiz. She had already begun to search for medical care for Rakan, the boy from Tal Afar who needed surgery, sending off e-mails to everyone she knew in the United States, looking for a doctor who would be willing to treat the boy. She even sent an e-mail to me. She stepped up the effort, using her military contacts to work on logistics to help evacuate the boy. And of course, Marla began visiting the families again. She worked on their claims forms, pushing for sympathy payments with a JAG at Camp Victory, located next to Baghdad International Airport (BIAP).

Tipped off by Chris Hondros's account in the *Times* of London, Marla also began talking to a high-ranking general about the military's civilian casualty records. She visited him at least once in the Green Zone and at least once at Camp Victory to discuss the issue. For the past three years, Marla had advocated for the military to keep a record of civilians it harmed. Until April 2005, she had come up empty.

Marla had disarmed the general with her compassion, commitment, and sense of fair play. He admitted that U.S. soldiers indeed filed reports whenever they injured or killed an innocent civilian. They had been doing so since the end of major combat operations on May 1, 2003.

Marla had discovered the tip of what was likely to be a mountain of civilian casualty data. Although her successes were many, it might have been the most significant achievement of her life. Some of the most experienced journalists in the world had neglected to uncover this story.

On April 9, Marla wrote an op-ed about the revelation and sent it to a Human Rights Watch friend and colleague for submission to newspapers back home. She encouraged the military to release these figures, as it would benefit the Iraqis and Americans alike.

COUNTING THE COST OF WAR

Baghdad, April 9, 2005

In my two years in Iraq, the one question I am asked the most is: "How many Iraqi civilians have been killed by American forces?" The American public has a right to know how many Iraqis have lost their lives since the start of the war and as hostilities continue. General Tommy Franks stated in a press conference in March 2003, "We do not do body counts." This outraged the Arab world and damaged the U.S claim of going to great lengths to minimize civilian casualties.

During the war, as U.S. troops pushed toward Baghdad, counting civilian casualties was not a priority for the military. However since May 1, 2003, when President George Bush declared major combat operations over and the U.S. military moved into a phase referred to as "stability operations," most units began to

keep track of Iraqi civilians killed at checkpoints or during foot patrols by U.S. soldiers. Here in Baghdad a Brigadier General
Commander explained to me that it is standard
operating procedure for U.S. troops to file a
spot report when they shoot a noncombatant. It
is in the military's interest to release these
statistics.

Recently I obtained statistics on civilian
casualties from a high-ranking U.S. military
official. The numbers were for Baghdad only,
for a short period, during a relatively quiet
time. Other hot spots, such as the Ramadi and
Mosul areas, could prove worse. The statistics
showed that 29 civilians were killed by small-
arms fire during firefights between U.S. troops
and insurgents between Feb. 28 and April 5,
four times the number of Iraqi police killed in
the same period. It is not clear whether the
bullets that killed these civilians were fired
by U.S. troops or insurgents.

A good place to search for Iraqi civilian
death counts is the Iraqi Assistance Center in
Baghdad and the General Information Centers
set up by the U.S. military across Iraq.
Iraqis who have been harmed by Americans have
the right to file claims for compensation at

these locations, and some claims have been paid. But others have been denied even when the U.S. was in the wrong.

The Marines have also been paying compensation in Falluja and Najaf. This data serves as a good barometer of the civilian costs of battle in both cities.

These statistics demonstrate that the U.S. military can and does track civilian casualties. Troops on the ground keep these records because they recognize they have a responsibility to review each action taken and that it is in their interest to minimize mistakes, especially since winning the hearts and minds of Iraqis is a key component of their strategy. The military should also want to release this information for purposes of comparison with reports such as the Lancet Study published late last year which suggested that the Americans were responsible for 100,000 deaths in Iraq.

A further step should be taken. In my dealings with U.S. military officials here, they have shown regret and remorse for the deaths and injuries of civilians. Systematically recording and publicly releasing civilian casualty numbers will assist in helping the victims who

survive to piece their lives back together. A
number is important not only to quantify the
cost of the war, but to me each number is also
a story of someone whose hopes, dreams and
potential will never be realized, and who left
behind a family.

Despite this groundbreaking triumph, Marla's emotional
strength began to wither again. The bipolar medication had
thrown her off-kilter, and she was having trouble sleeping.
She was also facing some financial problems, which led to an
argument with her mom, who was often annoyed by Marla's
struggles with paying rent and filing taxes. Further agitating
Marla's mental state, things were rocky with Phillip, to
whom she was still married. The April 15 income tax deadline was fast approaching, and Marla hadn't submitted the
necessary forms before she left for Iraq. They argued. Marla
loved Phillip, but she was angry and hurt. She attended a
birthday party one evening with Colin and other friends. At
one point the melancholy Cowboy Junkies song "Sweet
Jane" began to play, and Marla sang along to the bittersweet
lyrics. Before long, she was weeping openly. It had been a
difficult few weeks for many reasons, and several friends at
the party consoled her.

A few days later she went to see a military psychologist
and made up with her mom, and she seemed to be feeling
better. Some good news had come in: OSI had granted
CIVIC another sixty thousand dollars, once again throwing
her a financial life raft just when she needed it.

Marla had already stayed longer than the planned two weeks in Iraq. There were too many cases to follow up on, and she couldn't tear herself away quite yet. One of them was the medical evacuation of young Rakan. He had been languishing for nearly two months since he'd been shot in Tal Afar on January 18. By April 12, Marla had made some real progress. She had found both a doctor in San Francisco who would treat him and the finances to cover the cost of his travel. She wrote a desperate e-mail to a State Department official, begging for a fast-track humanitarian visa so the boy could receive treatment before it was too late.

On Thursday, April 14, Marla called Jon. A car bomb had exploded near the Hamra that day, leaving a burning wreckage of twisted steel and flesh in its wake, and she wanted to let him know that she was safe. She had started to forgive him and wanted to amend their friendship, planning to stop in London on her way back to New York. It was a quick chat—she was busy helping families—but she promised to call for a longer conversation over the weekend. Marla also left a message on her mom's cell phone, which Nancy listened to the next day: "Mom and Dad, I love you. I am safe." She also called Phillip, but like her parents, he missed the call.

The next day, April 15, Marla visited with the family that was perhaps closest to her heart. She hadn't forgotten Zahra, the three-year-old girl whom she and the army evacuated out of a Baghdad burn hospital in April 2003. She hadn't forgotten Zahra's family, either. When Zahra died, Marla had promised the girl's agonized grandmother that she would somehow find a way to help them, that they would not be forgotten. Marla kept her promise, eventually helping them win a five-thousand-dollar sympathy payment from the military.

April 16 would be another busy day for Marla. She had several meetings and visits planned and, like old times, a party to host at the Hamra that night. She sent Colin a couple of e-mails early that morning from the Convention Center in the Green Zone. The next time he heard from her was at around two p.m. She called to tell him that her "meeting" had gone really well. She sounded upbeat.

"I'll be back at the Hamra soon, but I've got one more thing I need to do," she told him. He was under the impression that she and Faiz were off to visit a family seeking a sympathy payment. He was rushing to complete a story and didn't have time to ask exactly where she was going.

At about six p.m., Colin tried to call Marla. He couldn't get a hold of her. It didn't strike him as odd; he figured she was dashing about making party arrangements. Several journalists who had been milling around the Hamra pool waiting for the hostess to arrive began to grow concerned. The hour was getting late.

Colin was still in his office, scrambling to file a story on deadline, when a colleague burst into the room.

"When's the party getting started?" Colin asked.

"Colin, Marla's not there. Nobody knows where she is."

He looked at his watch. It was eight o'clock. There was no way he wouldn't have heard from her by then.

His greatest fear seemed to be coming true: She'd been kidnapped. He abandoned his story and called the *Tribune's* security attaché, pulling him out of the shower. He called the kidnapping unit at the U.S. Embassy. Everyone joined in, frantically shouting into the phones, sending out an alert through Baghdad.

At about eleven p.m., Colin's security man called.

"I think I have some good news. There was a car accident, and a woman matching Marla's description was brought into the casualty hospital in the Green Zone and apparently she's stable."

Elated, Colin let everyone know the good news and headed back to his house. As he walked in, his cell phone rang. It was his security man again. Colin answered, looking out at the relieved faces of his friends who had gathered in the yard.

"It's bad, mate" was all he heard. With those three words, Colin knew.

He listened to his security man list the facts. A suicide bomber had blown up his vehicle next to Marla and Faiz's car on Airport Road at about three p.m. Shortly after the blast, Marla died. Later he would learn of her last words, spoken to an army medic on the pavement: "I'm alive." Unable to hear anymore, Colin hung up the phone. He looked up.

A friend caught his eye.

Seeing Colin's face, she knew too.

Cliff and Nancy were up early that Saturday morning. They had some business to take care of and were puttering around the office. A Lakeport police officer appeared in the reception area, and Cliff greeted him.

"Hi, Cliff. You better go get Nancy. I need to talk to you both."

Cliff brought Nancy from the back of the office, and they stood before the police officer. *Something's happened to Mark*, was the first thing Nancy thought.

"Please, I need you both to sit down," he said gently.

"This is the hardest part of my job. I'm so sorry. I don't know how to tell you this. Marla's been killed by a suicide bomber in Baghdad."

I drove along Lakeshore Boulevard, glancing at the address on a piece of paper in my hand. As I rounded a bend, a long row of parked cars lined the side of the road. It was April 22, the night before Marla's funeral service, when I parked my car on a grassy embankment beside the lake and walked toward the Ruzicka house, where Marla's parents were hosting the reception for close friends and family.

Nancy was standing out front greeting guests as they arrived. She was the perfect hostess, smiling and chatting.

Inside, a small table was set up in the corner where representatives from local wineries filled glasses. Locals recounted the lake's history to the growing crowd of out-of-town guests. I began putting faces to names I had heard countless times.

I bumped into a somber-faced Medea Benjamin near the kitchen. I introduced myself and we spoke briefly, interrupted by an announcement. An attractive woman with a diamond nose piercing asked for everyone's attention.

"Everyone, we just got word that Marla is about to arrive in Sacramento. We're going to have a moment of silence, so please be ready," said Jill, Marla's older half sister from their father's previous marriage, as she fought back tears. A few minutes later the lights were dimmed as Marla's body touched down on California soil, and we all bowed our heads. Nancy and Cliff stood upstairs alone, looking out across the lake toward Sacramento, crying.

Many journalists who knew Marla from Kabul and Baghdad began trickling in after the winding journey from San Francisco. Many were on the deck overlooking the lake, eating homemade tamales, drinking wine, and smoking cigarettes. I met Alfons Luna, the AFP journalist Marla lived with in Kabul and who had named his daughter after her. I had heard a lot about them; Marla often talked with glee about Nina and Alfons's little girl, Anna Marla. Adam Davidson from the Heatley dinner, whom I had met with Marla in Brooklyn two months before, was there too. I met Tara Sutton, the Canadian video journalist who had helped Marla in Baghdad. Nicole Boxer was there. Marla had talked excitedly about their wild night cruising through Manhattan in a limo that winter.

Jon Lee Anderson, the *New Yorker* correspondent, arrived as well and was talking to Marla's twin brother, Mark. Several of us stood by, listening to them talk about Honduras, where Mark lived off and on. He had curly, blond hair and the same cackling laugh as Marla, which sent chills up my spine.

I arrived at St. Mary Immaculate Church on Main Street an hour before Marla's funeral mass began. Tiny Lakeport had never received so much attention before. As many as a thousand people were expected to pay their respects. The church was already packed, with mourners lining the walls and spilling into a courtyard.

The pallbearers—Cat Philp, Marla's childhood friend

Colby Smart, Phillip, Tim Rieser, Peter Bergen, Tony Newman, Quil Lawrence, and Marla's godmother Eileen McGuire's daughter, Julie Pyzer—slowly began walking down the aisle. Bobby Muller, also a pallbearer, trailed behind in his wheelchair. As they passed by, I looked down at the pale oak coffin. I couldn't believe that Marla, so full of life, was in there. They continued to the front of the church, and the horrifying reality finally sank in.

After a sermon by Father Ted Oswald, who had known Marla since she was small, the eulogies began. It was the most powerful testament to a human being, living or dead, that I had ever heard. I was already well aware of Marla's unique personality and groundbreaking achievements, but nothing prepared me for the montage of heroic and hilarious stories. We journeyed with Marla from Lakeport to San Francisco; Zimbabwe to Afghanistan; Washington to Baghdad. Phillip coaxed a laugh out of the crowd when he described Marla salsa dancing in Zimbabwe when no salsa beat could be heard.

Along with Mark and the rest of the Ruzickas, Nancy and Cliff listened in the front pew. Their daughter was twenty-eight years old. I wondered if they had been fully aware of Marla's extraordinary influence on the world.

Tony Newman gave his second Lakeport address (the first had been on Cuba a decade before): "Marla saw the gift each person has to offer. Hers was that she could bring together soldiers, civilian victims of war, politicians, activists, and reporters. Marla taught us that when we recognize that we are all connected and that we all have gifts, we can change the world."

Medea Benjamin reminded us of Marla's diplomatic attributes: "If we lived in a more just world, Marla would be nominated to represent the United States to the United Nations. If Marla were the U.S. ambassador to the United Nations, I promise you this: America would be loved throughout the world," she said. She asked the family members of the Kabul September 11 delegation, who were among the mourners, to stand.

As Medea made her closing remarks, she invited a special guest to say a few words, and out of the blue, actor Sean Penn appeared on the podium. "I wish I had known your daughter, your sister, your friend. I count her as one of my heroes," he said before slipping off the stage.

Bobby Muller of the Vietnam Veterans of America Foundation gave one of the most powerful addresses of all.

"There's a lot of cynicism and hopelessness out there right now. People think there's nothing they can do. Marla demonstrated that a single individual can have a profound impact on the world. That's leadership. . . . In World War I, ninety-five percent of the casualties were soldiers. In World War II we firebombed cities and killed the innocent. The nature of warfare has changed. Today, ninety-five percent of the victims of war are civilians. . . . Marla managed to do in a few years what I haven't been able to achieve in thirty-five, and that's to prick the conscience of the American people. . . ."

Quil struggled to fight back his emotions as he made us laugh and cry at the same time. He summed Marla up perfectly: She was a cross between Mother Teresa and Buffy the Vampire Slayer. He took us on their road trip from Kabul to Mazar-i-Sharif, when Marla had shocked him by announcing that she hadn't brought a sleeping bag or any other survival gear. He told us that Marla would never forgive us if we didn't remember Faiz as well.

Cat also elicited laughter, recalling Marla's quirks: that she spilled and broke things; that she said "Yay!" with a little jump and clap when she was happy; that she called their friend Inigo "Indigo" by mistake; and that she left encouraging notes for friends, always dotting the letter *i* with a heart. Cat also discussed Marla's battle with depression.

Peter Bergen described the various phases of Marla's friendship: "I got the full Marla treatment. Phase one: 'Everyone says you're great.' Phase two: 'You're great. In fact, you're the most amazing person on the face of the Earth.' Phase three: 'Let me tell you about my work.' Phase four: 'How can you help?'" The church filled with laughter as many recalled identical treatment.

Senator Barbara Boxer, along with her daughter Nicole, also took their turn at the podium.

"It was Senator Leahy and Tim who were inspired to act by her courage, her cause, and the kindness and goodness that is Marla. Here was this young woman, who was sending a powerful message to Iraqis and Afghans that Americans were not going to turn their backs on them," Senator Boxer said.

Senator Boxer interrupted her eulogy to ask Tim to stand, emphasizing the tremendous part he personally played in Marla's life and in helping Senator Leahy pass the landmark legislation.

As the crowd applauded Tim, he covered his face with his hand and began to weep.

After the funeral mass, hundreds of friends packed into the

Ruzicka house and the neighboring yacht club. Everyone was mingling, drinking plenty of local wine, and nibbling on canapés. There were more tears, but most of all, there was laughter. Even in death, Marla was connecting the world, bringing people together in the name of love, throwing one last party.

The sky above the lake was cluttered with dark, billowy clouds that threatened to rain. We gathered on the lawn. Several held clumps of yellow balloons with messages for Marla written on their smooth surface. They were released, rushing toward the heavens. Just at that moment, the clouds parted. The sun peeked out and the balloons were swallowed up by a momentary slice of blue sky. And then, as quickly as it appeared, the sun was gone.

Over the next days and weeks, memorials were held all over the world for Marla: Baghdad, Kabul, San Francisco, New York, and at the Senate building in Washington. Two days after her death Senator Leahy eulogized her in an address on the Senate floor.

Later he took Marla's legacy all the way to the White House. At Senator Leahy's urging, President Bush signed legislation on May 11, 2005, which renamed the civilian war victims fund the "Marla Ruzicka Iraqi War Victims Fund." At the time of this writing, the combined sum that Congress has allocated to assist Afghan and Iraqi civilians who were victims of U.S. warfare is thirty-eight million dollars. Without Marla, the program never would have existed. It is a tragic irony that Marla herself became a civilian victim of war.

After Marla's death, there was no one left to organize Rakan Hassan's evacuation to the United States for surgery. A private citizen in Massachusetts read a news article about Marla's death—and that Rakan was left without hope for medical care as a result. Moved by the heartbreaking story, he wrote a three-line letter to Senator Edward M. Kennedy of Massachusetts, imploring him to help. The senator, also moved, took action. After a series of phone calls, conversations, and brainstorming sessions, the twelve-year-old boy was evacuated to the United States for medical care in September 2005. The military also awarded a sympathy payment of $7,500 to Rakan and his orphaned siblings.

However, others have yet to be helped. Arifa, Marla's friend from Kabul, was devastated when she heard on Afghan radio the news of Marla's death. To this day, Marla is the only person who tried to help her with compensation. Like everyone who knew Marla, Arifa lost more than a friend; she lost her hope that humanity can prevail in an often inhumane world.

But hope remains. Although it took some time to recover from the devastating blow, CIVIC has survived Marla and Faiz's deaths. Paperwork Marla neglected to file with the IRS was amended retroactively. A new director has been hired, and many of Marla's friends and colleagues—and even her mother—have pitched in to ensure that Marla's work continues to thrive.

When Marla was a budding activist volunteering for Global Exchange, she seized on the idea to write a "how-to" handbook for other young people who wanted to make a difference with their lives. Marla, of course, was too busy actually making a difference to see it through. In writing *Sweet Relief*, I've come to realize that Marla's life is that handbook.

May 14, 2006, Brooklyn

JENNIFER ABRAHAMSON

Acknowledgments

In true Marla form, the development of *Sweet Relief* was a communal effort; it never would have progressed beyond the book proposal she and I wrote together without the indispensable assistance provided me by her vast network of friends, colleagues, and relatives. Dozens of individuals went out of their way to help me piece together Marla's scattered movements into a coherent storyline, candidly sharing some of their most private memories. I thank each and every one of them for trusting me. But above all, I am indebted to Marla. She was a staunchly loyal friend who refused to give up on me when it would have been very easy to do so.

There are probably hundreds of friends and acquaintances of Marla's who I did not have a chance to interview. If I had spoken to each and every one of them, no doubt I would have spent many years of my life, and sacrificed several trees, to write this book. My hat goes off to those individuals whose timely help enabled me to write Marla's biography on my tight deadline—and under one thousand pages. I do not pretend that every detail of Marla's life has been explored in this text; rather, I have done my best within the parameters to illustrate who Marla was by recreating specific scenes from her life. I relied heavily on memory—my own, Marla's, and scores of others'—to reconstruct events and dialogue in this book.

The genesis of *Sweet Relief* was unusual. I would most likely still be working for the United Nations in Sudan, never to have written this book, if Justin Bishop at *Vanity Fair* had not referred me to *Elle* magazine's Alex Postman, who agreed to run my short profile on Marla in August 2004. Also, unbeknownst to David Wright, the idea of turning Marla's life into a book would not have been conceived without him. His *Nightline* piece gave Marla the boost she needed, as well as critical exposure in the United States, for which I am grateful. At around the time I wrote the *Elle* article, literary agent Joe Veltre met Marla in New York City. He had spent a year tracking her down after watching her on *Nightline* in mid-2003. Joe encouraged Marla to write her memoirs and she in turn proposed that I take on the challenge. My appreciation of Joe's hard work and patience runs deep. His dedication before and after Marla's death was instrumental in transforming this book from a dream to reality.

At Simon Spotlight, I am beholden to Publisher Jennifer Bergstrom for taking a chance on me, and for recognizing the truly awesome power of Marla's story. There are no adequate words to express my gratitude to Ryan Fischer-Harbage, who edited this book, other than: "You rock!" Ryan's skilled and tactful guidance, along with his unflinching support, to the point of rearranging his own life to see the manuscript to completion, made this a much better book than it would have otherwise been. Many thanks are also due to Terra Chalberg, who expertly picked up where Ryan left off, and to the brilliant team of copyeditors who cleaned up my careless mistakes.

It goes without saying that I am extremely grateful to Marla's family for granting me their blessing to carry on alone with the project she and I began in early 2005. The experience has been an honor and a privilege. Marla's parents, Nancy and Cliff Ruzicka, were incredibly brave in focusing on this book so soon after their daughter's death, as was her twin brother Mark. Nancy in particular was a great help in recounting Marla's childhood and putting me in touch with many sources in Lakeport. I am also thankful to Phillip Machingura, and to Marla's half-sister, Jill Leighton, for their backing, trust, diplomacy, patience, sympathetic ears, and, most of all, friendship.

Of the greater Lakeport community, I extend my appreciation to those who took the time and emotional energy to talk about their little girl, their best friend, their prized and idiosyncratic student. They are: the McGuire family, including Eileen (a special thanks for the champagne brunch), Laurie, Doreen, Julie and Pat; Colby and Toni Smart; Jim Rogers; Steve Gentry; Hillary Golden; Mr. and Mrs. Wilbur Facey; Erin Hagberg; Francesca Erickson; and Carol Magill.

I believe it was fate that led me to Christine Kozobarich at Marla's funeral service. Without Christine, reviving Marla's college years would have proved a fruitless task. Her kind words of encouragement and willingness to put up with my tedious questions and requests showed me why Marla chose her as a friend. Erin Gertz, Marla's closest college friend, demonstrated courage by speaking honestly and openly with me. I am convinced that Marla must have been proud of both women for dedicating their lives to helping others. Tami Farber also provided useful college information for this book.

Retracing Marla's steps in San Francisco, and recalling her professional experiences there, would have been impossible without the help of several people who carved time out of cluttered schedules to talk to me. Elizabeth Creely, one of Marla's truest friends, was a saint for agreeing to meet with me despite her protective instinct. She provided valuable insight into Marla's character, in effect improving my own understanding of her development. Of the current and former Global Exchange employees who worked and interacted with Marla, I am hugely grateful to Tony Newman, Michael Shellenberger, Kevin Danaher, June Brashares, Deborah James, and, above all, Medea Benjamin.

Without the assistance of many members of Marla's inner circle, including journalists, human rights experts, government officials, and military personnel, most of this book would be nothing but a collage of news articles thrown in with a smattering of my own memories. From Washington and Kabul to Baghdad and New York (and well beyond), each encounter, phone conversation, typed exchange, referral, and donated photograph enhanced my ability to do Marla's story a bit more justice. For their contribution, I would like to thank Thorne Anderson, Nicole Boxer, Kate Brooks, Stephanie Bunker of the United Nations Office for the Coordination of Humanitarian Affairs, Kelly Campbell of Peaceful Tomorrows, Massimo Casseriani, Julia Cohen, Lucy

Morgan Edwards, Jack Fairweather, Bay Fang, Inigo "Indigo" Gilmore, Ahmad Hashimi, Chris Hondros, Raed Jarrar, Mark Kukis, Richard Leiby, Rachel Levin, Rick Loomis, Colin McMahon, Bobby Muller of the Vietnam Veterans of America Foundation, Sergeant Dru Neason, Open Society Institute President Aryeh Neier, Jehad Nga, Sergeant Greg Papadatos, April Pedersen, Simon Robinson, His Excellency Omar Samad, Kimball Stroud, (former Army Captain) Jonathan Tracy, Jere Van Dyk, Robert von Dienes of the Open Society Institute, Vivienne Walt, Shaun Waterman, Ivan Watson, Edward Wong, David Wright (again), and Michael Zielenziger.

Several people involved in Marla's post-September 11 life went the extra mile in various capacities. I extend my sincerest thanks to Jon Lee Anderson of the *New Yorker* for taking the time to forward lengthy e-mail correspondence with Marla; for an especially illuminating interview; for writing *The Fall of Baghdad,* which served as a sacred resource on Iraq; and, most of all, for putting my mind at ease. Christina Asquith's ability to recall detail in vivid clarity astounded me. Without her, many passages from Marla's days in Iraq would have suffered in this book. I owe Jen Banbury and Adam Davidson drinks at a Brooklyn watering hole of their choice both for contributing fantastic material and for prying my cassettes from the hands of a particular Maryland resident. Which leads me to Nina Biddle and Alfons Luna, whose tape was mysteriously missing from the rescued batch. They whipped up a Spanish feast for me not once, but twice, seamlessly repeating their first heartfelt interview with tolerance and grace. Of Marla's many friends, they were among those who showed the most kindness.

Peter Bergen's thick stack of e-mails helped shed light on Marla's struggles, as well as on her frenzied movements. I thank him for sharing them, and for granting me his own blessing of sorts. Pam Constable of the *Washington Post* saved me more than she knows, not only by fleshing out important details about Jalalabad and Marla's time there, but by putting me in touch with Javed Hamdard in Kabul. Javed successfully located some of the Afghan victims that Marla helped, which lent a dimension to this book that it would have otherwise lacked. His journalistic acumen and patience are admirable. David Cory Frankel painstakingly detailed the birth of CIVIC—on the eve of the birth of his first child—and always responded to my pestering questions with lightning speed.

I have nothing but praise for Marc Garlasco and Sam Zia-Zarifi of Human Rights Watch. The arc of Sam's professional relationship and friendship with Marla stretched all the way from Kabul and Baghdad to New York. His insights were priceless. Marc's account of Marla's work in Iraq was particularly colorful. More important, I would have been lost somewhere between an AK-47 and a Kalashnikov without the lessons he imparted on warfare, the U.S. military's strategic maneuverings in Iraq, and the history of aerial bombing.

Quil Lawrence and Tara Sutton shared recorded material which helped me see Marla in action—and allowed her own voice to be "heard" in these pages. I also thank Quil for the reams of descriptive anecdotes he provided, and Tara, for directing me to Raed. Furthermore, I am very fortunate that

Tara always responded to my many irksome queries, whether she was just down the street or en route to Africa or the Middle East.

The opportunity to interview Catherine Philp and Jon Swain in person was well worth the trip to London. I am grateful to Jon for taking several hours to relive some very painful memories, and for braving the traffic-clogged streets of London to drive me home during a torrential rainstorm. Cat graciously set aside the better part of an unusually warm day during her short break between stints in Kabul and Baghdad to talk to me (sorry about the sunburn). This book would have lacked several critical layers without the dozens of personal e-mails she collated for me, and without her candid recollections of the final two years of Marla's life. I can't thank either of them enough.

Last, but certainly not least in the long line of this book's many sources, is Tim Rieser at the U.S. Senate. Despite his exceptionally busy schedule, Tim took time on more than one occasion to review passages of this book, and to explain the inner-workings of the policy-making process in Washington. Without his assistance, I would not have been able to accurately summarize Marla's groundbreaking achievements there.

On a personal note, I extend my thanks to Elisabeth Eaves for trusting me with her own book proposal, which served as an excellent guide; Susan Mindell for her legal wisdom; Cat Colvin for her lifesaving free counsel, and Marijana Wotton for putting me in touch with her (and for applying my makeup); Lora Davisson, without whose help I would not have been able to carry on; Kurt Pitzer for offering golden reporting advice; Keene Louis, Saheed Adebola, and Jonathan Olmo at Circuit City in Manhattan's Union Square for saving my life when my computer crashed two weeks before my deadline; the Brooklyn Writers Space for providing a quiet cubicle in which to toil; Adrian McIntyre for coming through in the end by assisting me with this book on more than one occasion; Irina Davidovich for her friendship and constructive criticism; Stefan Lovgren, whose brutal honesty finally came in handy; Marion Winik, whose speedy review of a first and partial draft of the manuscript put me on the right track; and to Christina Davidson, who early on lobbied for me despite the fact that we had just met, and for reading the penultimate manuscript at the final hour.

There are many friends and acquaintances who have withstood my griping and favor-seeking since this book project began. Katia Bennett and Tim Crowley, who provided a safe haven in Washington, D.C., went well beyond the call of duty, as did Connie Pollard and Laurent Samama, who graciously let me crash with them in London.

As for my family, Rob, Avi Rose, and Isaac "Spiderman" Perl have helplessly put up with my regular presence on their couch in Oakland over the past months and years, for which I thank them. My sister Amy's constant and unsolicited encouragement gave me the confidence to continue when I was convinced I would crumble under pressure. Along with Marla, I could not have asked for a more inspiring role model. My late grandparents, Charles and Dorothy Abrahamson, will never know just how much they have helped me. I would not have been able to write this book without them. I thank my father Michael for his generosity, tenacious support, and sage advice over the years, particularly in regards to writing *Sweet Relief*. Finally, I owe my life, in more than one way, to my mother Beverly Rose. She has borne the brunt of my darkest hours, especially since this project began. Without her I might not have pulled through.

Selected Reading

Anderson, Jon Lee, The Fall of Baghdad, New York: Penguin, 2004.

Ashley, Guy, MEDEA BENJAMIN Longtime S.F. Activist Finds the Humanitarian Angle in Politics," The Contra Costa Times, November 17, 2002.

Asquith, Christina, "What Iraqis Receive for Their Losses," The Christian Science Monitor, January 23, 2004.

Bearak, Barry, "Uncertain Toll in the Fog of War: Civilian Deaths in Afghanistan," The New York Times, February 10, 2002.

Carroll, Jill, "An American Activist who Dared to Help Iraqi Victims," Christian Science Monitor, April 18, 2005.

Carroll, Rory, "Pits Reveal Evidence of Massacre by Taliban—UN Team Visits Mass Graves for Proof of the Final Slaughter," The Guardian, April 8, 2002.

Carroll, Rory, "Bloody Evidence of US Blunder," The Guardian. January 7, 2002.

Cochrane, Joe, "Club Kabul; Afghanistan's Capital Finally Gets its Own post-Taliban Night Spot—and Opening is a Rave," Newsweek, February 26, 2002.

Collier, Robert, "It Takes Cash to Finish Job in Afghanistan," The San Francisco Chronicle, September 8, 2002.

Constable, Pamela, "A Disarming Presence in a Dangerous World," The Washington Post, April 19, 2005.

Constable, Pamela. Fragments of Grace: My Search for Meaning in the Strife for South Asia. Virginia: Potomac Books, 2004.

Cullen, Kevin, "Rakan's War," The Boston Globe, February 26, 2006.

Davidson, Adam, "Out of Iraq," Harper's, February 2005.

Gall, Carlotta, "Shattered Afghan Families Demand US Compensation," The New York Times, April 8, 2002.

Jaber, Hala, "You Can Help Save a Child Victim of War—The Sunday Times Merlin Appeal—Iraq," The Sunday Times, April 20, 2003.

Jarrar, Raed, "Raed Remembers Marla," Guerrilla News Network, April 21, 2005.

Kong, Deborah, "Mourners Gather for Arab-American Who May be Hate Crime Victim," The Associated Press, October 4, 2001.

Landler, Mark, "Sharing Grief to Find Understanding," The New York Times, January 17, 2002.

Lum, Lydia, "Group Defies Blockade, Returns from Cuba," The Houston Chronicle, July 1, 1995.

Mangaliman, Jessie, "Many Work to Erase Anger at Muslims," The San Jose Mercury News, September 29, 2001.

Ostrowski, Jeff, "Green Party Observers Have to Stand at Recount," The Palm Beach Post, November 16, 2000.

Otton, Chris, "US Embassy in Kabul Recommends Compensation for Afghan War Victims," Agence France-Presse, April 7, 2002.

Pearson, Bryan, "Afghan Victims of US Bombings Demand Compensation," Agence France-Presse, February 13, 2002.

Reitman, Valerie, "Afghan Journey Eases a Father's Pain War," The Los Angeles Times, January 22, 2002.

Reuters, "US Group Assessing Civilian Costs of Afghan Bombing," Reuters, February 14, 2002.

Robertson, Phillip, "Marla Ruzicka, RIP," Salon, April 18, 2005.

Seierstad, Asne, A Hundred and One Days: A Baghdad Journal, New York: Perseus, 2005.

Sengupta, Kim, "As the Bombs Continue to Fall, Another US Aircraft Lands in Afghanistan," The Independent, January 16, 2002.

Shanker, Thom, "US Changes Guidelines for Troops to Lessen Everyday Tensions with Iraqi Civilians," The New York Times, May 2, 2006.

Sly, Liz, "Iraq Blames Missile Strikes for 14 Deaths," The Chicago Tribune, March 27, 2003.

Sullivan, James, "Seeking Solace in the Arts," The San Francisco Chronicle, September 17, 2001.

Swain, Jon, "B-52s Rain Hellfire on the Villagers of Kama Ado," The Sunday Times, December 9, 2001.

Walt, Vivienne, "Aid Must Pass Through Wall of Suspicion; Troops Try to Help Villagers without Alienating Them," USA Today, April 14, 2003.

Worth, Robert F., "An American Aid Worker Is Killed in Her Line of Duty," The New York Times, April 18, 2005.